Bethany S. Reynolds

STARS
A LA CARTE

WITH
MAGIC
STACK-N-WHACK™
BONUS
PROJECTS

American Quilter's Society

P. O. Box 3290 • Paducah, KY 42002-3290

Located in Paducah, Kentucky, the American Quilter's Society (AQS) is dedicated to promoting the accomplishments of today's quilters. Through its publications and events, AQS strives to honor today's quiltmakers and their work and to inspire future creativity and innovation in quiltmaking.

EDITOR: BARBARA SMITH
BOOK DESIGN: TOM SULLIVAN
ILLUSTRATIONS: BETHANY S. REYNOLDS
COVER DESIGN: MICHAEL BUCKINGHAM
PHOTOGRAPHY: CHARLES R. LYNCH

Library of Congress Cataloging-in-Publication Data
Reynolds, Bethany S.
    Stars a la carte : with magic stack-n-whack bonus projects / Bethany S. Reynolds.
       p. cm.
    Includes bibliographical references.
    ISBN 1-57432-739-9
    1. Patchwork--Patterns. 2. Quilting--Patterns. 3. Star quilts. I. Title.
TT835 R4594 2000
746.46'041--dc21   00-020756

Additional copies of this book may be ordered from the American Quilter's Society, PO Box 3290, Paducah, KY 42002-3290 @ $21.95. Add $2.00 for postage and handling.

Contents

Dedication

To Bill and Sam,

the two bright stars in my life –

*thanks always for your love,
understanding, and encouragement.*

Acknowledgments

✧ *Many thanks to Meredith Schroeder and the staff at the American Quilter's Society for their continued faith and support and their help in creating this book. A special thank you to Barbara Smith, for her graciousness as well as her meticulous editing skills.*

✧ *I'm grateful to my students and the many Internet quilters who provided valuable feedback on my instructions, with special recognition to Mary Schilke and Hilary Gray.*

✧ *I am indebted to Eleanor Flathers for inspiring the "Magic Mirror Image Trick," which I am sure will send legions of quilters on a fabric scavenger hunt; and to Linda Worland of Paper Panache for sharing her "Butterfly Trick."*

✧ *To the Wednesday Weasels, my local quilt gang, thanks for your willingness to try anything I ask of you with humor and patience. Save me a cookie. I'll be back next week.*

Introduction

The Block We Love to Hate

Whether called the LeMoyne Star, Lemon Star, or any of its many other aliases, few designs have occupied a place of honor in quiltmaking for as long as the Eight-Pointed Star. This simple arrangement of eight diamonds has delighted quilters for more than two centuries, but its origins go back much further. Across time and geographical boundaries, from ancient Rome and the Renaissance to our own quilting traditions, the Eight-Pointed Star appears time and again.

Eighteenth- and nineteenth-century quilters probably enjoyed this block for its economy as well as its graphic impact. The traditional block has just three easily drafted templates: a diamond, a triangle, and a square. These pieces can be cut from scraps or yardage with little waste. As long as these pieces are carefully drawn and cut, the block is fairly simple to piece by hand.

But quilters who prefer machine piecing have long felt confounded by Eight-Pointed Stars. The "Y" seams formed by the diamonds and background squares are a challenge even for experienced piecers. More than a few quilters have surrendered after battling pleated intersections, misaligned centers, and blocks that refuse to lie flat no matter how much coaxing they receive at the ironing board.

This book takes a different approach to the Eight-Pointed Star. With the addition of a few strategic seams, this temperamental block takes on a much more cooperative demeanor.

Divide and Conquer

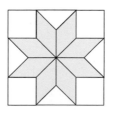

Botanists create new hybrids to take advantage of the strengths of the parent plants. What might happen if we apply the same principle to quilt blocks? Suppose we take the classic Eight-Pointed Star block and cross-pollinate it

with a block that is very simple to piece, such as the humble four-patch Pinwheel block?

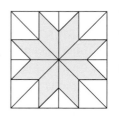

What we have now is a new block that combines the graphic appeal of the Eight-Pointed Star with the ease of construction of the Pinwheel block.

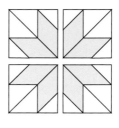

Thanks to the four-patch Pinwheel construction, we can piece this block in four identical quarters.

Each quarter is made from two half-square triangle units.

The half-square triangle units consist of a diamond and two different sized triangles.

This new block has a few more seams than the one our foremothers pieced by hand and uses a little bit more fabric because of the additional seam allowances. However, for machine piecers, this is a fair trade-off for the elimination of those set-in "Y" seams.

Now that we have the basic block, we can have some fun with variations. Simple changes in fabric placement can lead to new blocks that are as easy to sew as the basic star.

Introduction

By adding pieces to the diamond on each point of the star, we can create new block designs like these.

These new variations may look difficult to piece, but paper piecing makes those sharp points manageable. Several of the star blocks in this book are sewn using a method I call "partial paper piecing." In many paper foundation piecing projects, the paper is left in place until the block is completed, and sometimes until the entire top is pieced. I have found this unnecessary for these blocks. In the directions given in this book, the paper foundation used to assist in piecing the diamond units is removed during the block construction.

Finally, by choosing a dynamic setting to complement the star blocks, we can show off this timeless design in all its splendor! This book offers a variety of interesting settings. Each features a particular block design, but you can substitute any of the other blocks for your own customized design.

How to Use This Book

This book provides instructions for making the quilts shown in the photo plates, and additional information to help you design and create your own unique quilt. Yardages and cutting instructions are given for both 6" and 12" block sizes. You can use any block variation with any Quilt Plan, giving you a great many options for projects of various sizes, from very small wall quilts to bed quilts. You can also tailor the difficulty of the project to your needs by using the skill ratings given for each block and Quilt Plan.

The Fabric Selection chapter offers tips on choosing fabrics to make your star quilts sparkle.

Part One provides instructions for the star blocks. Each block design chapter includes the cutting and piecing directions for the diamond star points. The Star Block Piecing chapter gives step-by-step directions for adding

the background fabric to the diamonds and completing the block. This part includes a special section on using the Stack-n-Whack™ technique to create stars with kaleidoscopic effects.

Part Two provides plans for a variety of settings. Each Quilt Plan includes a yardage chart, cutting charts for the background and accent fabrics, and piecing instructions for the setting. Since you may choose to use a different star block from the one shown in the sample for the Quilt Plan, the instructions will refer you to Part One for the block piecing directions.

If you would like to customize your quilt by substituting different blocks or borders for those shown in the sample quilts, Part Three provides information to help with this.

Part Four includes a General Instructions section for techniques used in the book that may be new to you, including the partial-paper-piecing technique. You will also find suggestions for quilting and finishing your project in this section.

In the last pages of the book, you'll find the paper foundations to copy for the star blocks, and quilting and appliqué designs.

Understanding the Illustrations

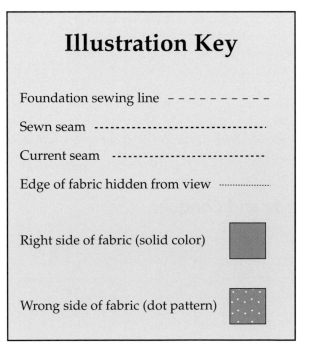

Illustration Key

Foundation sewing line – – – – – – – –

Sewn seam ·····································

Current seam ·····························

Edge of fabric hidden from view ················

Right side of fabric (solid color)

Wrong side of fabric (dot pattern)

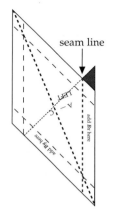

seam line

• The piecing illustrations are oriented to show the fabric unit as it is being sewn. The seam line will be vertical and on the right-hand side.

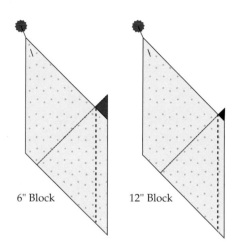

6" Block   12" Block

• The block piecing illustrations show the 6" blocks. The seam allowances will be proportionately smaller in the 12" blocks.

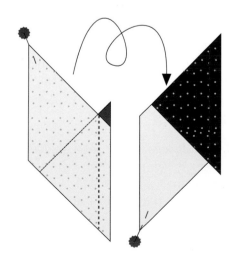

• For the paper piecing steps, the new fabric patch must be underneath so that the printed line is visible. For the conventional piecing steps, some quilters prefer to piece

with the new fabric patch on top, and some prefer it on the bottom. It does not matter which method you use, as long as the unit matches the illustration after sewing and pressing.

If an illustration seems backward to you, try placing the fabric exactly as shown and then flip it to the sewing position that feels right for you.

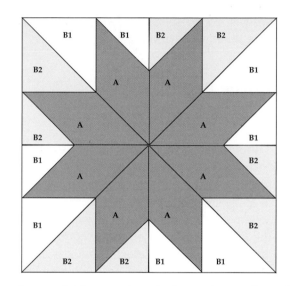

• Background fabric is identified as Fabric B throughout. If there are two background fabrics in the block, they are identified as B1 and B2.

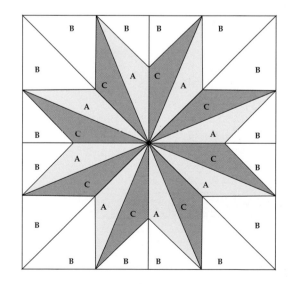

In blocks with two star fabrics, Fabric A is shown as a lighter shade, and Fabric C is shown as a darker shade. You do not need to adhere to these positions, but remember this when you follow the illustrations if you choose to switch them.

Fabric Selection

Selecting fabrics is always a key step in making a sensational quilt. Quilters all have individual approaches to this process, and we may find we need to vary our tactics for certain designs. For these star quilts, you may want to try a somewhat unorthodox approach.

Start at the Back

Why begin with the background fabric?

The stars should be the focal point of these quilts. However, the star points actually occupy only a small area of the design. To keep them in the foreground, you will want to select a background fabric that complements them without competing for attention. The background fabric will be the largest yardage used in the quilt, and it is frequently the most difficult to select. I find it is often easier to choose the background fabric first and then select the star-point fabrics. This is particularly true for quilts with scraps or multiple fabric combinations in the star blocks.

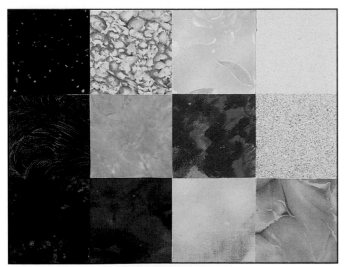

Photo 1: Examples of good background fabrics.

For star blocks that have a single background color, look for a background fabric that will disguise the seam lines so the blocks will appear to "float" in the background. Where the background of a star block meets the background in an adjacent setting block, a fabric that hides the seam will create an impression of more space around the star.

Photo 2a   Photo 2b

In the left photo, the busy background competes with the star. The right photo shows better contrast.

Photo 3a   Photo 3b

In the left photo, the random stripe has a distracting effect. In the block on the right, the stripes are cut and placed to frame the star.

Look for a background fabric with subtle variation and low contrast in the design, such as the textured designs, hand-dyed fabrics, and soft marbled prints shown in Photo 1. Avoid busy or high contrast prints which may detract from the stars (Photos 2a and 2b). Stripes and other directional fabrics may require special attention for best effect (Photos 3a and 3b). Keep scale in mind as well. Prints that may work beautifully with 12" stars might overwhelm the 6" stars.

Black and other dark solids are good choices for dramatic quilts (see STRIPE IT RICH, page 80). Light solids will show the seams more than prints or dark solids, but they are good choices if you plan to do elaborate quilting in the background areas.

For star blocks with two-color or scrap-style backgrounds, keep in mind that the star points should stand out against the background fabrics. To play it safe, choose fabrics for the background that are close in value, such as the cream and light tan shades shown in TURN OF A DIFFERENT CENTURY (page 45) or the light background prints used in YANKEE THRIFT (page 68). Use strong contrast in the background fabrics only if you have a star fabric that can hold its own, such as the bold print used in the cover quilt.

Shining Stars

Because the star points require fairly small amounts of fabric, these blocks are ideal for playing with fabric combinations and showing off special pieces from your stash. You can use a single fabric combination in all the star blocks or a variety of combinations for a scrap effect. In Part One, you will find specific tips for each block, but here are some general suggestions:

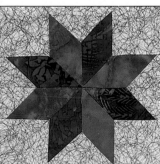

Photo 4a Photo 4b
Small-scale prints and solids are easy to control.

Photo 5a Photo 5b
Large prints, such as this batik, may produce unintended effects when cut. In this block, the star tips nearly disappear into the background.

Look for good contrast between the star fabrics and the background. Smaller prints and solids offer dependable results (Photos 4a and 4b). The types of prints shown in Photo 1, shown on page 8, for background fabrics will also work well for star points. Large-scale prints are less predictable. They may appear light in one diamond and dark in another, especially in the smaller blocks (Photos 5a and 5b).

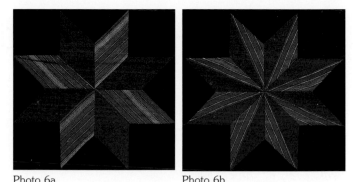

Photo 6a Photo 6b
Striped star-point fabrics will have different effects, depending on the block design.

Stripes can be used in some of the blocks. The effect will be quite different depending on the block design. In the basic blocks, the grain line runs parallel to one edge of the diamond. Stripes will shift in direction around the points (Photo 6a). In the Split Star block, the grain line runs up the center of the diamond. Stripes will radiate out from the center (Photo 6b).

Accent Fabrics

Some of the quilt plans call for additional fabrics in the setting or border. You can choose to repeat the star fabrics in these positions, or select additional fabrics to complement your background and star-point fabrics. The choices for these may be quite flexible. If possible, piece some of the star blocks before selecting the remaining fabrics. Seeing the relative strength or softness of the stars in a finished block will help you select appropriate accent fabrics.

One More Thought

Even if you are a novice quilter, don't be afraid to use the nicest fabric you can afford. A beautiful fabric will give you a great head start on a beautiful quilt!

Basic Eight-Pointed Star Block

Skill Level, 6" Block: Easy
Skill Level, 12" Block: Easy

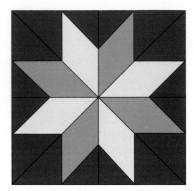

Using two alternating colors in the star points draws attention to the center of the block, emphasizing perfect piecing. Novice quilters may want to choose the more forgiving one-color star for a first try. Scrap-fabric stars are especially fun to make if you have a generous selection of fabrics in your collection.

These basic stars work nicely in all of the Quilt Plans. If you are a novice quilter, you can substitute them for the more challenging star blocks shown in some of the samples to simplify the project.

Star Fabric requirements are included in the Quilt Plans and listed separately in the Star Fabric Yardage Charts on page 85.

Cutting the Star Diamond Fabrics

If you plan to make all the stars alike, follow the cutting instructions for the total number of stars you desire. For one- or two-color stars with different fabrics in each block, use the "1 Star" instructions to cut the fabrics for each star.

Rotary cutting instructions for 45° diamonds are on page 93.

6" Star Blocks

Cutting Diamonds for 6" One-Color Star					
	1 Star	5 Stars	6 Stars	8 Stars	12 Stars
Cut this many 1¾" strips across width:	1	3	4	5	7
Cut strips into this many 45° diamonds (1¾" slices):	8	40	48	64	96

Cutting Diamonds for 6" Two-Color Star					
	1 Star	5 Stars	6 Stars	8 Stars	12 Stars
Cut this many 1¾" strips across width from each fabric:	1 (12" long)	2	2	3	4
Cut strips into this many 45° diamonds (1¾" slices) from each fabric:	4	20	24	32	48

Cutting Diamonds for 6" Scrap Star					
	1 Star	5 Stars	6 Stars	8 Stars	12 Stars
Cut this many 45° diamonds (1¾" slices) from assorted fabrics:	8	40	48	64	96

12" Star Blocks

Cutting Diamonds for 12" One-Color Star					
	1 Star	5 Stars	6 Stars	8 Stars	12 Stars
Cut this many 3" strips across width:	1	5	6	8	12
Cut strips into this many 45° diamonds (3" slices):	8	40	48	64	96

Cutting Diamonds for 12" Two-Color Star					
	1 Star	5 Stars	6 Stars	8 Stars	12 Stars
Cut this many 3" strips across width from each fabric:	1 (20" long)	3	3	4	6
Cut strips into this many 45° diamonds (3" slices) from each fabric:	4	20	24	32	48

Cutting Diamonds for 12" Scrap Star					
	1 Star	5 Stars	6 Stars	8 Stars	12 Stars
Cut this many 45° diamonds (3" slices) from assorted fabrics.	8	40	48	64	96

Star Block Piecing

Basic Eight-Pointed Stars

For the one-color, two-color, and scrap stars, cut the diamonds according to the appropriate charts on pages 10–11. Divide the diamonds for one block into two piles, one for the left and one for the right pieced diamond units. The illustration shows the pieces for a two-color star, with the lighter color used for the left units and the darker color for the right units. Place a reference pin at the center tip of each diamond. The pin will help you keep the piece oriented correctly as you follow the piecing illustrations.

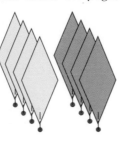

Whirligig, Compass, and Split Stars

Piece the diamond units according to the directions for each block. Keep the left and right units separate.

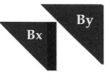

LEFT   RIGHT

Crazy Eights

Piece the diamond units and label them according to the directions (pages 30–32). Follow the illustrations for the basic star, noting the position of the center tip in each illustration.

Background Triangles

For all the star blocks, cut the background fabric triangles according to the charts in the Quilt Plan chapters or use the reference charts on pages 87–88. The smaller triangles are the Bx triangles, and the larger ones are the By triangles. The illustrations show the one-color background triangles for one block. Keep the two sizes in separate piles.

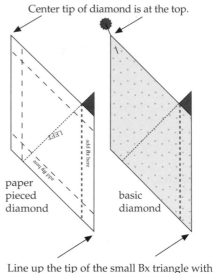

Center tip of diamond is at the top.

paper pieced diamond   basic diamond

Line up the tip of the small Bx triangle with the outer tip of the diamond.

Begin with the left diamonds. For the basic diamonds and the Crazy Eight diamonds, turn the diamonds so that the pins are at the top as shown.

For the other paper pieced diamonds, turn the diamond so that the edge that reads "add Bx here" is on the right. With right sides together, sew a small (Bx) triangle to the lower right edge of each diamond, lining up the lower corner of the background triangle with the outer tip of the diamond. The corner of the Bx triangle should extend ¼" at the beginning of the seam as shown.

STOP *Do Only the 4 Left Diamonds!*

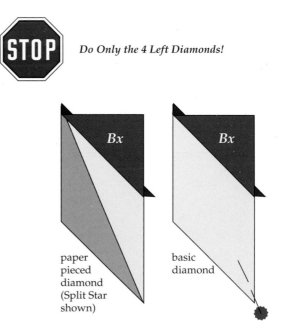

paper pieced diamond (Split Star shown)   basic diamond

Press the allowances toward the background, taking care not to stretch the bias edges.

Line up these straight edges.

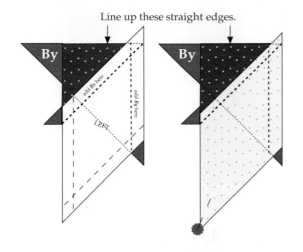

Turn the diamonds so that the center tips are at the bottom. With right sides together, sew a large By triangle to the upper-right edge of each diamond. The straight top edges of the Bx and By triangles should line up. The corner of the By triangle should extend ¼" at the bottom of the seam as shown.

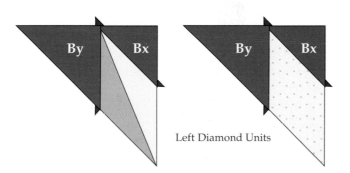

Left Diamond Units

Press the allowances toward the background, taking care not to stretch the bias edges. For the basic stars, remove the reference pins.

Line up the small Bx triangle with the outer tip of the diamond.

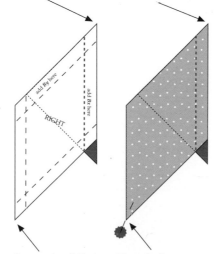

Center tip of diamond is at the bottom.

Now, piece the right diamonds. For the basic diamonds, turn the diamonds so that the pins are at the bottom as shown. For the paper pieced diamonds, turn the diamond so that the edge that reads "add Bx here" is on the right. With right sides together, sew a Bx triangle to the upper-right edge of each diamond, lining up the upper corner of the background triangle with the outer tip of the diamond. The corner of the Bx triangle should extend ¼" at the bottom of the seam, as shown.

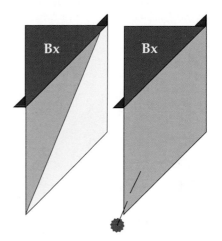

Press the allowance toward the background, taking care not to stretch the bias edges.

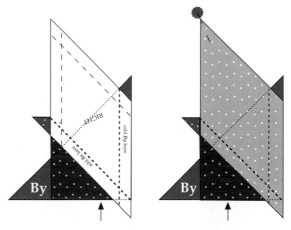

Line up these straight edges.

Turn the diamonds so that the center tips are at the top. With right sides together, sew a By triangle to the lower-right edge of each diamond. The straight bottom edges of the Bx and By triangles should line up. The corner of the By triangle should extend ¼" at the beginning of the seam as shown.

Piecing the Blocks

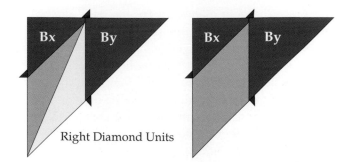

Right Diamond Units

Press the allowance toward the background, taking care not to stretch the bias edges. For the basic stars, remove the reference pins.

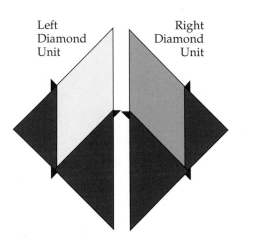

Left Diamond Unit

Right Diamond Unit

Place the left and right diamond units together in pairs.

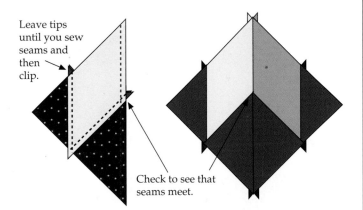

Leave tips until you sew seams and then clip.

Check to see that seams meet.

Sew left and right diamond units together to make quarter blocks. Be sure to carefully match the seams between the background fabric and the diamonds. Clip the triangle tips along the seam. Press these seam allowances open.

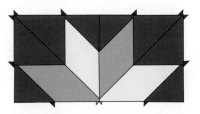

Sew the quarter blocks together in pairs, matching the crossed seams at the center (see Getting Those Centers to Come Out Right, below). Clip the triangle tips along the seams. Press the seam allowances open.

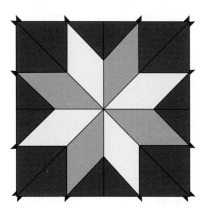

Sew the half blocks together, matching the seams at the center. Clip the tips, and press the center seam allowances open.

Getting Those Centers to Come Out Right...

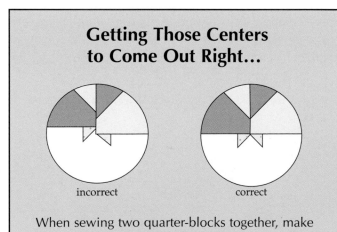

incorrect   correct

When sewing two quarter-blocks together, make sure the seams meet ¼" in from the edge, as shown in the figure on the right. If they don't match up now, they won't match up later!

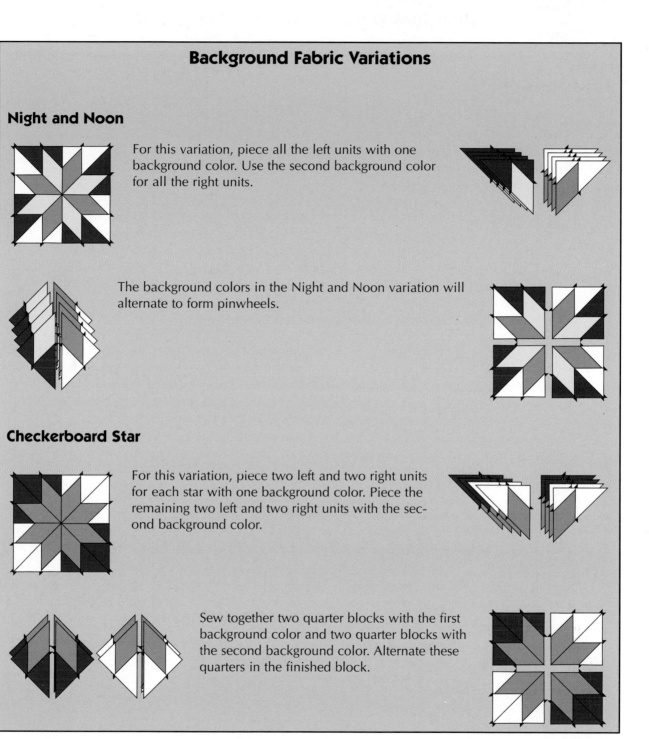

Background Fabric Variations

Night and Noon

For this variation, piece all the left units with one background color. Use the second background color for all the right units.

The background colors in the Night and Noon variation will alternate to form pinwheels.

Checkerboard Star

For this variation, piece two left and two right units for each star with one background color. Piece the remaining two left and two right units with the second background color.

Sew together two quarter blocks with the first background color and two quarter blocks with the second background color. Alternate these quarters in the finished block.

When Should the Foundations Come Off?

Many paper piecing directions recommend leaving the foundations in place until the entire quilt top is pieced. This method helps to stabilize the edges, but the paper can make the top stiff and difficult to handle.

- You can remove the foundations from both diamonds after adding the background triangles and before sewing the quarter blocks. Removing the foundations at this point in the piecing process is easier, because there are fewer seams. This method offers a good compromise between the accuracy of foundation piecing and the simplicity of conventional piecing.

- Some quilters prefer the stability provided by leaving the paper in place, and they like having a printed seam line to follow. However, having two or more layers of fabric sandwiched between two layers of paper creates a lot of bulk that might interfere with the feed-dog action on some sewing machines. One solution is to remove the paper from the bottom piece only (in this case, the left diamond). Removing just the bottom piece allows the machine to feed more evenly and reduces the chance of pieces shifting, and you will still have a seam line to follow on the top layer.

- The star blocks will lie flatter if the seam allowances that come together in the center of the block are pressed open during construction. Pressing is much simpler to accomplish with the paper removed. Small pieces of paper will not get buried under the seam allowances, and you will have the option of pressing the seams with an iron without the risk of smearing ink from the foundation. If you choose to leave the foundations in place, tear away the sections in and beside the seam allowances before pressing them open.

- Removing the paper before joining pieces may expose some off-grain edges to possible distortion. As with conventional piecing, careful handling and pinning can minimize problems.

- There are no laws regarding paper piecing. Experiment to find the approach that works best for you.

How to Remove the Foundations

- Grip the beginning of a seam between thumb and forefinger to prevent the stitching from pulling out.

- Tug gently across the area from which you are removing the paper. The paper should begin to tear along one of the seam lines.

- Tear the foundation away carefully, keeping your finger grip next to the tearing line.

- Smaller pieces may be easier to remove if you tear away larger adjacent areas first.

- Acids in paper will deteriorate fabric if left in contact with it for extended periods. If you want to give your finished quilt a longer life span, remove all traces of paper from the seams. You may want to use tweezers to remove the smallest bits.

Stack-n-Whack™ Variations

The Stack-n-Whack method, introduced in *Magic Stack-n-Whack Quilts* (see Bibliography, page 127), is an easy way to create blocks with unique kaleidoscope designs. Eight-Pointed Star blocks produced with this method can be used in any of the Quilt Plans in this book. This section reviews the procedure for preparing (stacking) and cutting (whacking) the fabrics to make 45° diamonds.

Stack-n-Whack Fabric Requirements

If you choose to use Stack-n-Whack stars in place of the basic or paper pieced stars shown in the Quilt Plans, substitute the star fabric yardage requirements given here. The background and setting fabric requirements will not change.

Almost any printed fabric with a regular repeat can be used for Stack-n-Whack projects. For more dramatic results, look for lively prints with a variety of shapes, lines, and colors. Medium- to large-scale prints are recommended for the 12" stars, but even small-scale prints can be effective for the 6" blocks.

Since the pieces for Stack-n-Whack blocks are cut from lengthwise repeats, the fabric requirements will vary according to the repeat length of the print. A length of eight design repeats will produce enough blocks for any of the Quilt Plans, in either 6" or 12" block sizes. If you choose a fabric with a longer repeat, you will have more left over.

Finding and Cutting the Repeats

The repeats are cut from a single layer of fabric. For accuracy and ease of handling, work with one half of the fabric width to cut the repeats for each stack. This will be about 21" if the fabric is 42" wide. Fold the fabric with selvages together to find the center, or measure 21" from one selvage. Cut or tear along the lengthwise grain for about a yard. Fold the remaining fabric out of the way and square off the cut end of the fabric (Photo 7).

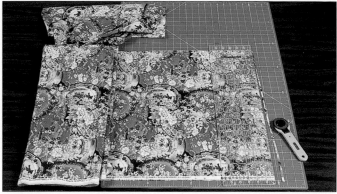

Photo 7

Switch the bulk of the fabric to your right if you are right-handed (or to your left if you are left-handed). Smooth out the squared-off end of the fabric on your cutting mat. Examine the selvage of your fabric near the squared-off end and find a motif close to the edge. Move your eyes along the selvage until you find the same motif, in the same orientation. Measure between these two points to find the length of the design repeat. This will be the length of your guide piece (Photo 8).

Photo 8

Note: If you are using a border stripe with various patterns, measure the lengthwise design repeat on different parts of the stripe. If the measurements vary, the safest approach is to use the full printing repeat length, which is usually identifiable along the selvage by the printed brand name or color registration dots.

Star Fabric Requirements – Stack-n-Whack Variation
6" or 12" Star Blocks

(Measurements in yards unless otherwise indicated.)

If the Design Repeat of Star Fabric is	6"–10"	11"–14"	15"–20"	21"–27"	over 27"
You will need this many yards	2½	3½	5	6¾	8 repeats

Piecing the Blocks

Photo 9

Measure from the straightened edge along each side to the length you have established for the guide piece. Mark the length with rotary cuts (Photo 9).

Photo 10

Line up your ruler with the cut marks and cut across the width to make the guide piece (Photo 10).

Photo 11

With selvages and cut edges aligned, lay the guide piece on the remaining fabric so that the print matches exactly. Smooth out the guide piece and use your fingertips to match up the design all across the cut edge that is nearest to the remaining uncut fabric. The edge should nearly disappear as it lines up with the print on the lower, uncut layer (Photo 11).

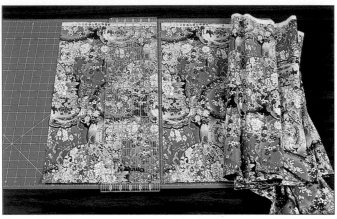

Photo 12

When you have it matched exactly, lay your ruler down along the edge and cut across (Photo 12).

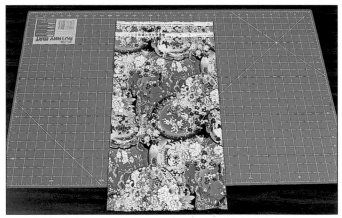

Photo 13

You now have two identical print rectangles (Photo 13). Set one piece aside. Cut or tear along the length of the fabric, if necessary, and smooth out the portion you are cutting. Use the guide piece again to cut a third repeat and set it aside.

Photo 14

Repeat this process until you have eight repeats, including the guide piece (Photo 14). Be sure to cut all these repeats from the same half of the fabric. Printing and finishing processes can cause slight distortions even in high quality fabrics, and the differences may be noticeable in the finished blocks if you use crosswise, rather than lengthwise, repeats.

Stacking the Layers

You now have eight identical layers, each one repeat long. Take the layers one at a time and press them lightly. If you've prewashed the fabric, you may want to use a little sizing or spray starch to return some crispness to the fabric, which will make the pieces easier to handle and will help keep bias edges from stretching.

Stack the layers, smoothing each piece so that the selvages and cut edges line up. When you have all the layers stacked, you can use a method I call "stick-pinning" to position them accurately. You'll need one pin with a large round head, and several flower-head pins. These are long pins with a large flat head that will not interfere with the

Photo 15

ruler. If you do not have these, you can use long pins with small metal heads. These are harder to see, though, so take extra care to keep stray pins out of the way of your cutting blade.

To "stick-pin" fabric layers, select a point on the fabric design about 2" in from the selvages and 1"–1½" from the cut edge. Look for something that's distinctive and easy to spot, such as the tip of a leaf. Place the tip of the round-headed pin on this spot. Lift the top layer of fabric, sliding the tip of the pin through. Find the same point on the next layer and slide the pin through. Continue lifting layers and pinning through this point until you have gone through all the layers (Photo 15).

Photo 16

Slide the pin all the way through to the head and hold it in place with your thumb and forefinger. Hold the pin straight up and down and smooth out the surrounding fabric. Take a flower-head pin and pin across through all the layers, right beside the stick pin (Photo 16).

Remove the stick pin. Lay the fabric down flat and repeat the pinning process at three other points across the width. The extra time spent in careful pinning now will pay off later in more accurate blocks.

Whacking the 45° Diamonds

Once you have stacked the layers, cut strips through all eight layers and cut 45° diamonds from the strips. The Stack-n-Whack Cutting Charts on page 21 indicate the number of strips needed for various numbers of blocks. The following photos show the 1¾" diamonds used in the 6" star block.

Piecing the Blocks

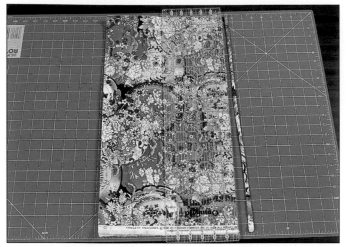

Photo 17

Trim the stack along the pinned crosswise edge to ensure a straight edge through all the layers (Photo 17).

Photo 18

Turn the stack around or rotate the mat. Cut a strip through all the layers, using the strip width measurement given in the Stack-n-Whack chart on page 21 (Photo 18).

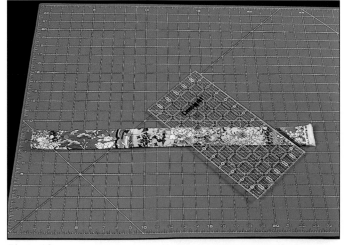

Photo 19

Place the 45° line of the ruler along one edge, close to the selvage, and cut (Photo 19).

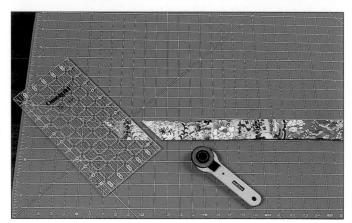

Photo 20

Turn the strip set and again place the 45° line along one edge. Measure over from the angled edge, using the same measurement as the strip width. Cut to make a 45° diamond. This makes one block kit (the set of eight identical diamonds needed for one block) (Photo 20).

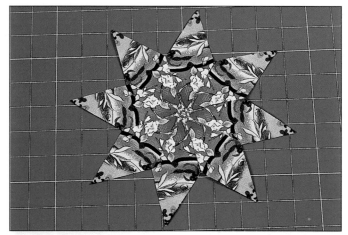

Photo 21

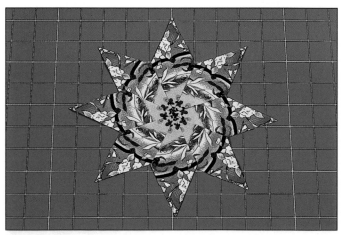

Photo 22

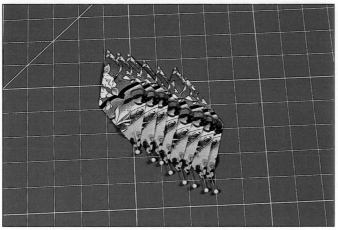

Photo 23

Continue cutting diamonds, removing pins as you go. If two or more strips are needed, repin the stack and trim if needed to get an even edge before cutting each strip. The charts on this page indicate the number of strips needed for various numbers of block kits.

The 45° diamonds can be used with either tip at the center. You may want to lay out the pieces and preview the block both ways before sewing (Photos 21 & 22, page 18).

Once you have decided which tip you would like in the center, place a reference pin at that end of each diamond in the block kit (Photo 23).

Follow the basic eight point star piecing directions (pages 12–14) to piece the block.

Stack-n-Whack Cutting Charts

Follow the directions on pages 17–20 to prepare the stack. Cut strips and diamonds for your project according to the following charts.

Piece the star blocks following the instructions for the basic star (pages 12–14), including background variations, if desired.

Stack-n-Whack Chart for 6" Star Blocks			
Guide Piece . . .	Stack . . .	Whack . . .	To make. . .
21" wide x one full repeat long	8 identical layers of star fabric	21" x 1¾" strips	45° diamond block kits (7 per strip)
For 5–6 blocks, cut one strip. For 8–12 blocks, cut two strips.			

Stack-n-Whack Chart for 12" Star Blocks			
Guide Piece . . .	Stack . . .	Whack . . .	To make. . .
21" wide x one full repeat long	8 identical layers of star fabric	21" x 3" strips	45° diamond block kits (4 per strip)
For 5–8 blocks, cut two strips. For fabrics with a repeat under 7", you will need a second stack from the remaining width; cut 1 strip from each stack. For 12 blocks, cut three strips. For fabrics with a repeat under 9", you will need a second stack; cut 2 strips from the first stack and 1 strip from the second.			

Piecing the Blocks

SUMMER SOLSTICE by author, 1999. The Magic Mirror-Image Trick adds classic symmetry to these Stack-n-Whack™ stars. This quilt is set in the Stargazer Quilt Plan on page 55, using 12" blocks.

The Magic Mirror-Image Trick

If you have the good fortune to find a certain type of fabric print, you can achieve some astonishing effects by using the Magic Mirror-Image Trick with the Stack-n-Whack method. Any extra effort will be spent fabric shopping, rather than cutting and piecing. The secret lies in finding a main fabric that is printed so that the front and reverse sides are almost indistinguishable.

Fabrics that work well for this trick are hard to find in cotton quilting fabric. They are more common in poly/cotton fabrics, especially lightweight polished chintz types. Test potential fabrics by folding the reverse side over to the front and checking each color, one by one. Prints with light backgrounds are more likely to work. The two sides do not have to be identical to get the mirror-image effect. Slight variations will not be very noticeable in the finished block and may even add a subtle dimension to the design.

To get the Magic Mirror-Image effect, stack all the layers right side up. Cut the diamonds as directed for the basic Stack-n-Whack star. No special placement is necessary, because any part of the design will produce a unique mirror image.

After you lay out the diamonds for each block, flip over every other one so the reverse side is up. Place pins in the center tips. Stack the diamonds in two piles – the reverse diamonds in one pile and the front side diamonds in the other. Piece as for the basic star, using the pins as a reference.

Stars a la Carte – Bethany S. Reynolds

The Magic Mirror-Image Trick

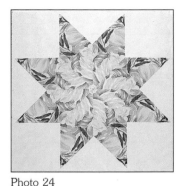

Photo 24

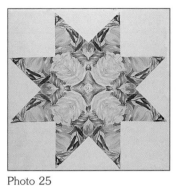

Photo 25

In the left photo, all the diamonds are right side up. In the right photo, every other diamond has been reversed to create the mirror image effect.

Paper Pieced Diamond Variations

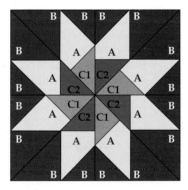

Whirligig Star Block

Skill Level, 6" Block: Easy
Skill Level, 12" Block: Easy

This simple block accommodates a wide variety of fabric choices. The A triangles, which form the star tips, should have some value or color contrast with the background fabric. The C triangles, which form the whirligig in the center of the block, are shown with two alternating colors. For a one-color version, cut twice the number of triangles listed in the chart from a single fabric.

The On-Point and Diamond Border Quilt Plans complement the simple charm of the Whirligig Star block. The Night and Noon and Checkerboard settings offer interesting possibilities, too. Experiment with different color placements in the star tips, whirligigs, and background fabrics.

Star fabric requirements are included in the Quilt Plans and listed separately in the Star Fabric Yardage Charts on page 85.

Pre-Cutting the Star Diamond Fabrics

To simplify the paper piecing process, pre-cut the pieces for the star diamonds. If you plan to make all the stars alike, follow the cutting instructions for the total number of stars you desire. For Whirligig Stars with different fabrics in each block, use the "1 Star" instructions to cut the fabrics for each star.

Piecing the Blocks

Pre-Cutting Star Fabric for 6" Whirligig Star Diamonds					
	1 Star	5 Stars	6 Stars	8 Stars	12 Stars
Cut this many 3" strips across width from Star Tip Fabric A:	1 (12" long)	2	2	3	4
Cut strips into this many 3" squares:	4	20	24	32	48
Cut each square once on the diagonal to make this many triangles:	8	40	48	64	96
Cut this many 2½" strips across width from each Whirligig Fabric (C1 and C2):	1 (5" long)	1	1	1	2
Cut strips into this many 2½" squares of each fabric:	2	10	12	16	24
Cut each square once on the diagonal to make this many triangles of each fabric:	4	20	24	32	48

Pre-Cutting Star Fabric for 12" Whirligig Star Diamonds					
	1 Star	5 Stars	6 Stars	8 Stars	12 Stars
Cut this many 4¾" strips across width from Star Tip Fabric A:	1 (19" long)	3	3	4	6
Cut strips into this many 4¾" squares:	4	20	24	32	48
Cut each square once on the diagonal to make this many triangles:	8	40	48	64	96
Cut this many 4" strips across width from each Whirligig Fabric (C1 and C2):	1 (16" long)	1	2	2	3
Cut strips into this many 4" squares of each fabric:	2	10	12	16	24
Cut each square once on the diagonal to make this many triangles of each fabric:	4	20	24	32	48

Paper Piecing Whirligig Star Diamonds

Piece Four Left and Four Right Diamonds for Each Block

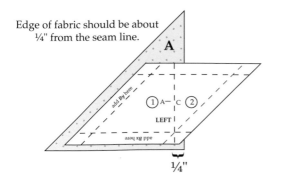

Edge of fabric should be about ¼" from the seam line.

Hold the paper foundation for the left diamond unit with the printed side facing you and the stitching line between pieces A and C running vertically, as shown. Place a triangle of Star Point Fabric A against the unprinted side of the paper, with the wrong side of the fabric against the paper. The triangle should cover the A area on the left side of the foundation and extend ¼" past the seam line for C. Hold the triangle in place with a pin or a dab of glue stick.

Fold the foundation over along the seam line. Place a triangle of Whirligig Fabric C1 under the Fabric A triangle

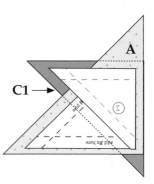

as shown, right side facing up. Note that the folded top layer of the foundation (shown in white) is lying over the C1 triangle. The triangle should line up with Fabric A along the seam line. It should extend beyond the outlines of the folded part of the foundation on the other two edges so that it will cover area C after sewing.

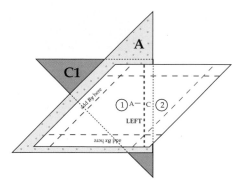

Fold the foundation out flat. Stitch along the line, beginning and ending at the outer cutting lines.

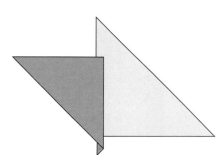

Turn the foundation over and press the C1 triangle open flat.

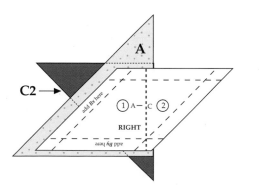

Piece the right diamond unit in the same manner, using C2 for the whirligigs.

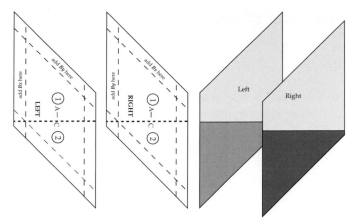

Trim along the solid outer cutting lines to complete the diamond units.

The quarter-blocks may look odd, but they are correct!

Continue piecing the block, following the Star Block Piecing instructions, pages 12–14. The quarter-block unit should look like this.

Piecing the Blocks

Split Star Block

Skill Level, 6" Block: Intermediate
Skill Level, 12" Block: Intermediate

Fabric choice is critical to the effectiveness of this block. The block is most striking when there is strong contrast between the star points (Fabrics A and C) and between the points and the background. The star points may contrast in color as well as value. For example, they can be a light blue and a dark green or they can be two shades of the same color.

With a very dark background, light and medium star points have a chance to shine. If the background is medium in value, choose very dark and very light fabrics for the star points. Light backgrounds are a little harder to use effectively. Medium and dark star points may lack the "sparkle" of the other combinations. If you prefer to use a light background, try using a fairly light medium fabric with a darker fabric.

Solids and tone-on-tone or other low-contrast prints will produce more dramatic stars, while multicolored or high-contrast prints may lend a softer appearance. Lengthwise striped fabrics can be used for one or both star points.

The versatile Split Star block works well in the Stargazer, On-Point, and Diamond Border Quilt Plans. The Night and Noon and Checkerboard settings are also options, provided the two background colors are chosen carefully so that they do not compete for attention with the star points.

Star Fabric requirements are included in the Quilt Plans and listed separately in the Star Fabric Yardage Charts on page 85.

Pre-Cutting the Star Diamond Fabrics

To simplify the paper piecing process, pre-cut the pieces for the star diamonds. In the piecing illustrations, A is the lighter fabric and C is the darker fabric.

If you plan to make all the stars alike, follow the cutting instructions for the total number of stars you desire. For Split Stars with different fabrics in each block, use the "1 Star" instructions to cut the fabrics for each star.

Pre-Cutting Star Fabric for 6" Split Star Diamonds					
	1 Star	5 Stars	6 Stars	8 Stars	12 Stars
Cut this many 4¾" strips across width from each fabric (A and C):	1	2	2	2	3
Cut strips into this many 1¼" x 4¾" rectangles of each fabric:	8	40	48	64	96

Pre-Cutting Star Fabric for 12" Split Star Diamonds					
	1 Star	5 Stars	6 Stars	8 Stars	12 Stars
Cut this many 8" strips across width from each fabric (A and C):	1	2	3	4	5
Cut strips into this many 2" x 8" rectangles of each fabric:	8	40	48	64	96

Stars a la Carte – Bethany S. Reynolds

Paper Piecing Split Star Diamonds

Piece Four Left and Four Right Diamonds for Each Block

Place a rectangle of Fabric A and one of Fabric C together with right sides facing.

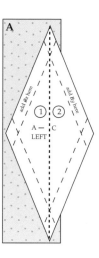

Lay the left diamond foundation on top of Fabric A as shown, with the printed side of the paper facing up and the wrong side of Fabric A facing the unprinted side of the paper. Place the center seam line ¼" to the left of the fabric edge, and center the seam line along the length of the rectangle. Stitch on the line, beginning and ending at the outer cutting lines.

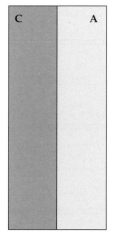

Turn the foundations over and press the C rectangles open.

Piece the right diamonds in the same manner.

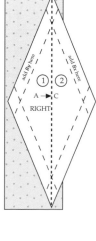

Trim along the solid outer cutting lines to complete the diamond units. The left and right diamonds should look the same when the fabric side is facing up.

Continue piecing the block, following the Star Block Piecing instructions, pages 12–14.

A Special Note for the Split Star Block

This star is simple to piece, but a challenge to piece perfectly. Take care when sewing the quarter blocks to make sure all the seams meet as closely as possible at the ¼" seam line. Because so many seams come together in the center of the block, sewing the last seam to complete the block may pose a challenge for you and your machine. If your machine does not handle multiple thicknesses well, you may prefer to hand sew the center 1" or so of this seam. If you choose to sew it by machine, here are some tips:

• Press the two halves as flat as possible. Make sure the seams that are pressed open remain open throughout the piecing to distribute the bulk.

• Use a sharp needle with a size 14 or larger eye. Quilting, jeans, or top-stitching needles work well.

• As the presser foot approaches the center, it will slant upwards over the bulk of the seams. Apply pressure to the front of the foot with a fingertip to help level the presser foot. You may need to "walk" the foot over the seam by taking a stitch at a time until you are past the bulky area.

• Finger press this last seam allowance open, and then lay a damp press cloth over the seam and press with the iron.

Piecing the Blocks

Compass Star Block

Skill Level, 6" Block: Advanced Intermediate
Skill Level, 12" Block: Intermediate

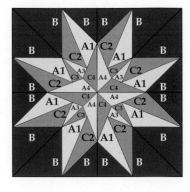

See the fabric suggestions for the Split Star block (page 26). Strong contrast, especially in value, will enhance the three-dimensional illusion of the Compass Star. Stripes are not recommended for this block because they will not always radiate from the center, due to the paper piecing order.

This dramatic block is very effective in the Stargazer Quilt Plan or any of the Diamond Border settings. Note that the compass points will appear tilted in the On-Point Quilt Plan.

Star Fabric requirements are included in the Quilt Plans and listed separately in the Star Fabric Yardage Charts on page 85.

Pre-Cutting the Star Diamond Fabrics

To simplify the paper piecing process, pre-cut the pieces for the star diamonds. In the piecing illustrations, A is the lighter fabric and C is the darker fabric. There are three different sizes of rectangles, and each size should be cut from both A and C.

If you plan to make all the stars alike, follow the cutting instructions for the total number of stars you desire. For Compass Stars with different fabrics in each block, use the "1 Star" instructions to cut the fabrics for each star.

Pre-Cutting Star Fabric for 6" Compass Star Diamonds					
	1 Star	5 Stars	6 Stars	8 Stars	12 Stars
Cut this many 1¼" strips across width from each fabric (A and C):	1	4	4	6	8
Cut strips into this many 1¼" x 3¼" rectangles of each fabric:	8	40	48	64	96
Cut this many 1⅛" strips across width from each fabric (A and C):	1 (7" long)	1	1	2	2
Cut strips into this many 1⅛" x 1¾" rectangles of each fabric:	4	20	24	32	48
Cut this many 1½" strips across width from each fabric (A and C):	1 (12" long)	2	2	3	4
Cut strips into this many 1½" x 3" rectangles of each fabric:	4	20	24	32	48

Pre-Cutting Star Fabric for 12" Compass Star Diamonds					
	1 Star	5 Stars	6 Stars	8 Stars	12 Stars
Cut this many 2" strips across width from each fabric (A and C):	2	6	7	10	14
Cut strips into this many 2" x 5¾" rectangles of each fabric:	8	40	48	64	96
Cut this many 1½" strips across width from each fabric (A and C):	1 (12" long)	2	2	3	4
Cut strips into this many 1½" x 3" rectangles of each fabric:	4	20	24	32	48
Cut this many 2¼" strips across width from each fabric (A and C):	1 (18" long)	3	3	4	6
Cut strips into this many 2¼" x 4½" rectangles of each fabric:	4	20	24	32	48

Paper Piecing
Compass Star Diamonds

Piece Four Left and Four Right Diamonds for Each Block

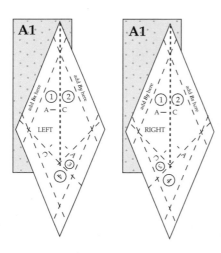

Begin with an A1 patch and a C2 patch. (The numbers refer to the area that will be covered.) These are the longest rectangles of each color. Place them with right sides together.

Lay a diamond foundation on top of A1 as shown, with the printed side of the paper facing up and the wrong side of A1 facing the unprinted side of the paper. Place the center seam line ¼" to the left of the fabric edge and center the seam line along the length of the rectangle. Stitch along the line, beginning at the outer cutting line and ending

one or two stitches beyond the point where the three seam lines cross. Repeat this step for all eight diamonds.

Fold the foundations along the C seam line on each diamond, extending the crease to the edges. Trim the A1 and C2 patches ¼" from the fold.

Turn the foundations over and press the C2 patches open to cover area #2. Be careful to avoid tucks in the seam line, so that the inner and outer points will be accurate.

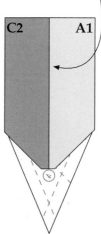

Make sure there are no tucks in this seam!

Piecing the Blocks

Separate the left and right diamonds for the following steps.

Left Diamonds

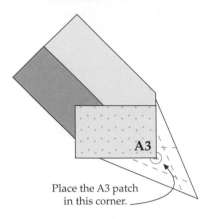

Place an A3 patch (the smallest A rectangle) over these pieces, right sides of fabric together. The rectangle should line up with the trimmed edges of the A1 and C2 patches as shown.

Place the A3 patch in this corner.

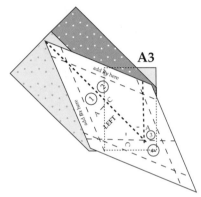

Flip the unit over so the foundation is on top. Stitch along the line, beginning at the outer cutting line and ending just beyond the C4 seam line.

Press the A3 patch open to cover area #3, taking care to avoid tucks.

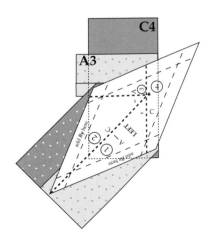

Place a C4 patch (the widest C rectangle) under the foundation, right sides of fabric together. The rectangle should line up with the trimmed edge of A1. It should be placed so that it will cover area C4, including the seam allowances.

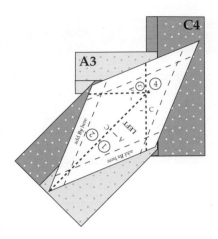

Stitch on the line, beginning and ending at the outer cutting lines. Press the C4 patch open.

Right Diamonds

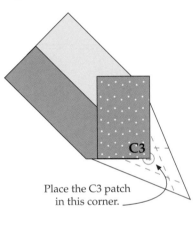

Place a C3 patch (the smallest C rectangle) as shown, right sides of fabric together. The rectangle should line up with the trimmed edges of the A1 and C2 patches.

Place the C3 patch in this corner.

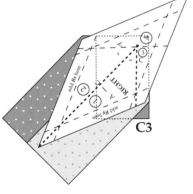

Flip the unit over so the foundation is on top. Stitch along the line, beginning just before the A4 seam line and ending at the outer cutting line.

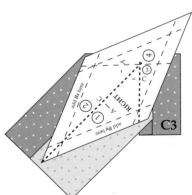

Press the C3 patch open, taking care to avoid tucks.

Stars a la Carte – Bethany S. Reynolds

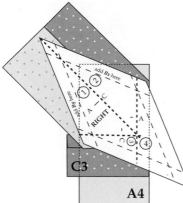

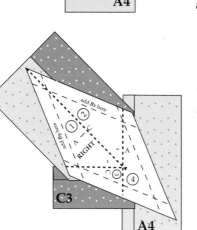

Place an A4 patch (the widest A rectangle) under the foundation, right sides of fabric together. The rectangle should line up with the trimmed edge of C2. It should be placed so that it will cover area A4, including the seam allowances.

Stitch on the line, beginning and ending at the outer cutting lines. Press the A4 patch open.

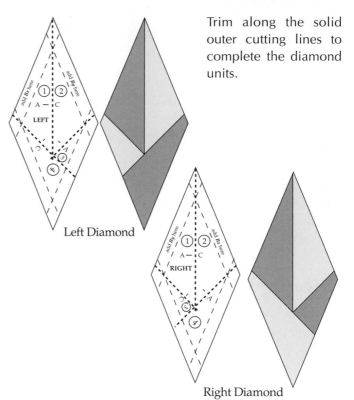

Left Diamond

Right Diamond

Trim along the solid outer cutting lines to complete the diamond units.

Continue piecing the block, following the Star Block Piecing instructions, page 12. The A3 and C3 tips should match in the quarter-block units, as shown. The A4 and C4 tips should match when the quarter blocks are sewn together to make half blocks.

Crazy Eights Block

Skill Level, 6" Block: Intermediate
Skill Level, 12" Block: Easy

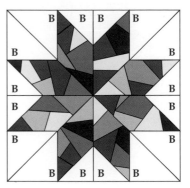

This block is ideal for using small cuts of fabric or scraps. Use many different fabrics for a good crazy-quilt effect. Be sure to pick a background fabric that will provide a good contrast in color or value to the crazy pieced stars.

These busy blocks generally look best in simple settings. The On-Point Quilt Plans are nice with or without appliqué in the alternate blocks. The Diamond Border Quilt Plans, using Crazy Eights diamonds, are also very effective.

Star Fabric requirements are included in the Quilt Plans and listed separately in the Star Fabric Yardage Charts on page 85.

Pre-Cutting Star Diamond Fabrics

For easier handling, precut each fabric you plan to use in strips. The strips can vary in width and length, but a 2"-wide strip will cover any of the patch areas on the 6" block, and a 3" wide strip will cover any of the areas on the 12" block. Initially, you can cut one or two strips from each fabric. Cut additional strips as needed.

Paper Piecing Crazy Eights Diamonds

Follow the illustrated instructions for paper piecing the Crazy Eights diamonds. Piece a set of eight different diamonds for each block.

Paper Piecing Crazy Eights Diamonds

The illustrations show the Crazy #1 foundation used for the 6" Crazy Eights block. If you are not experienced at paper piecing, try this diamond first so that you can follow the illustrations. For a practice diamond, you will need six scraps, each about 2" wide and 2"–3" long.

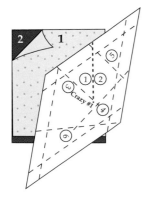

Place two different patches of fabric right sides together and lay the foundation on top as shown, with the printed side of the paper facing up and the wrong side of fabric #1 facing the unprinted side of the paper. Place the seam line between the #1 and #2 patches ¼" to the left of the fabric edge, and place the seam line along the length of the rectangle so that the fabric will cover each of the areas.

Stitch along the seam line. The stitching should begin and end one or two stitches beyond the point where another seam line crosses. If the printed seam line continues to the cutting line of the foundation, stitch all the way to the outer edge.

Turn the foundation over and fold the #2 fabric over to cover area #2. Finger press the seam line (see Pressing Issues, page 95).

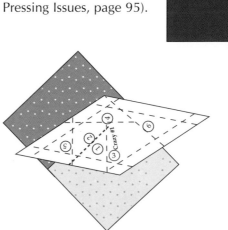

Flip the piece over so that the foundation is on top, and turn it so that #3 is upright.

Fold the foundation along the #3 seam line, extending the crease to the edges. The paper may not lie completely flat at the point where the previous stitching line extends into area #3. Trim the fabric #1 and #2 scraps ¼" from the fold with a rotary cutter or scissors.

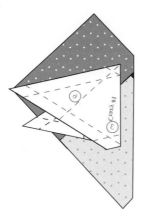

Turn the foundation so #4 is upright and fold along the #4 seam line, extending the crease to the edges. Trim the excess fabric ¼" from the fold.

Place a strip of fabric #4 under the foundation, right sides of fabric together. As before, the strip should line up with the trimmed edges of the previously sewn pieces and extend above the beginning of the seam line. This piece will be nearly hidden from view. The edges are shown by the dotted line. Hold the pieces up to the light if necessary to check the position.

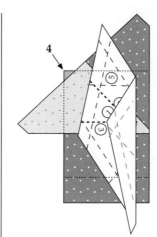

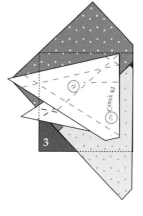

Place a strip of fabric #3 under the foundation, right sides of fabric together. The strip should line up with the trimmed edges of the previously sewn pieces and extend above the beginning of the seam line. With the foundation still folded over, check the size of the next area (see The Butterfly Trick, page 96). The hidden edges of the fabric piece for area #3 are shown with a light dotted line.

Fold the foundation back out flat and stitch along the line.

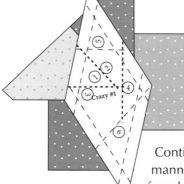

Fold the foundation back out flat. Stitch along the printed line.

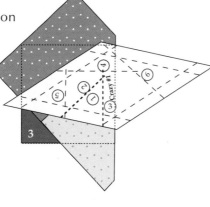

Finger press the fabric over to cover area #4.

Continue to add patches in this manner until all the areas of the foundation have been covered.

Finger press the fabric open to cover area #3.

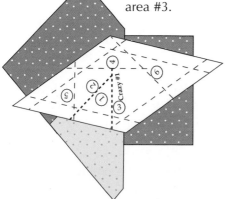

In some cases, you may need to tear the foundation a bit along a sewn seam line to allow it to fold back flat for trimming, as shown here.

tear here

Piecing the Blocks

These illustrations show the remaining piecing steps for the sample diamond.

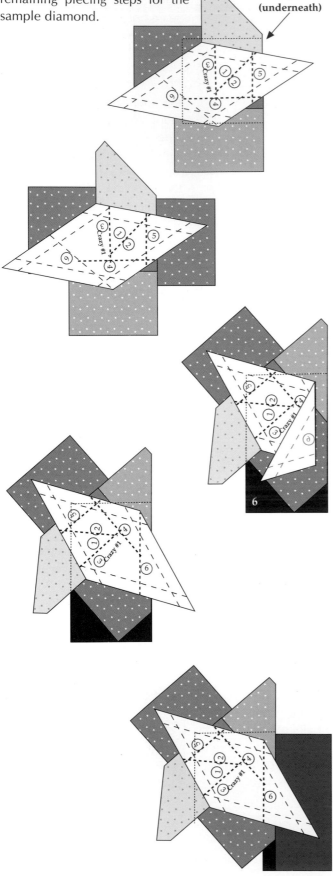

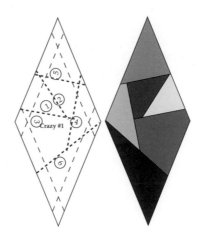

Trim along the solid outer cutting lines to complete the diamond unit. Piece the other foundations in the same manner.

Piecing the Crazy Eights Block

These diamonds can be used with either end at the center of the block, and they do not need to be placed in the original numerical order within the block. Varying fabric placement and diamond placement from block to block will create a more interesting crazy-quilt effect. Lay the completed diamonds for each block out on a flat surface to determine the arrangement you prefer.

Turn the diamonds over and label them on the paper side as a piecing reference. Label the center tip of each diamond and number the outer tips in order from 1–8.

Continue piecing the block, following the Basic Star Piecing Instructions. Use all the diamonds you labeled with odd numbers for the left units, and the even numbered diamonds for the right units.

If desired, add blanket stitching or embroidery to the finished blocks.

Stars a la Carte – Bethany S. Reynolds

WASTE NOT, WANT MORE by author, 1998. A hoarded stash of Cherrywood Fabrics hand-dyed cotton scraps inspired this quilt. Insufficient yardage for a single-color binding provided a creative opportunity. The pieced binding is the result.

Quilt Plans

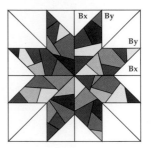

On-Point Quilt Plans with Six Stars

WASTE NOT, WANT MORE

See page 35
Skill Level with Basic Star Blocks: Intermediate
Finished Quilt with 6" Blocks: 21" x 29½"
Finished Quilt with 12" Blocks (shown): 42" x 59"

Fabric Requirements		
(Measurements in yards unless otherwise indicated)		
	6" Blocks	**12" Blocks**
Background Fabric	1⅜	2½
Fabric for Crazy Eights blocks*: assorted scraps totaling at least	½	⅞
Appliqué Fabric (opt): one color or assorted	¼ or (6) 7" squares	¾ or (6) 13" squares
Narrow Border	¼	⅜
Binding	⅜	½
Backing	1	2¾
*To substitute a different block, refer to the Star Fabric Yardage Charts on page 85.		

Star Blocks

Prepare diamond units for six Crazy Eights blocks (pages 32–34) or for the star block of your choice, following the cutting and piecing instructions in Part One.

Cut the background fabric for the star blocks.

Cutting Background Fabric for Star Blocks			
Block Size	**First Cut**	**Second Cut**	**Cut each square once on the diagonal to make...**
6"	(2) 2⅛" strips across width	(24) 2⅛" squares	(48) **Bx** triangles
	(2) 2⅝" strips across width	(24) 2⅝" squares	(48) **By** triangles
12"	(2) 3⅜" strips across width	(24) 3⅜" squares	(48) **Bx** triangles
	(2) 4⅜" strips across width	(24) 4⅜" squares	(48) **By** triangles

Piece six star blocks.

Alternate Blocks and Optional Appliqué

Cut the outer borders and alternate blocks from the background fabric, following the chart below. Note that the alternate blocks are cut slightly larger for the appliquéd version.

If you are using appliqué in the setting blocks, complete the appliqué before assembling the top. Follow the general instructions for machine appliqué in Part Four (pages 99–100) or use your favorite method.

For the appliqué, trace two complete wreaths for the center blocks, six half wreaths for the side blocks, and four quarter wreaths for the corner blocks. Place them on the background fabric following the instructions with the appliqué design on pages 99–100. Complete the appliqué. Trim the blocks as directed on the appliqué design page.

Cutting Outer Borders and Alternate Blocks from Background Fabric		
Block Size	**First Cut**	**Second Cut**
6"	(4) 2" x 27" strips cut lengthwise for outer borders	(2) 6½" squares* from remaining fabric for alternate blocks
	(2) 9¾" squares* from remaining fabric	Cut each square twice on the diagonal to make (6) side triangles, plus 2 extras
	(2) 5⅛" squares* from remaining fabric	Cut each square once on the diagonal to make (4) corner triangles
12"	(4) 3½" x 56" strips cut lengthwise for outer borders	(2) 12½" squares* from remaining fabric for alternate blocks
	(2) 18¼" squares* from remaining fabric	Cut each square twice on the diagonal to make (6) side triangles, plus 2 extras
	(2) 9⅜" squares* from remaining fabric	Cut each square once on the diagonal to make (4) corner triangles

* For appliquéd version, cut these squares 1" larger. Trim after completing the appliqué (pages 99–100).

Assembling the Quilt

Arrange the star and setting blocks, following the Quilt Assembly Diagram. Sew the seams in each diagonal row, then sew the diagonal rows together.

Cutting Inner Borders	
Block Size	**Cut**
6"	(4) 1" strips across width
12"	(5) 1½" strips across width

Quilt Plans

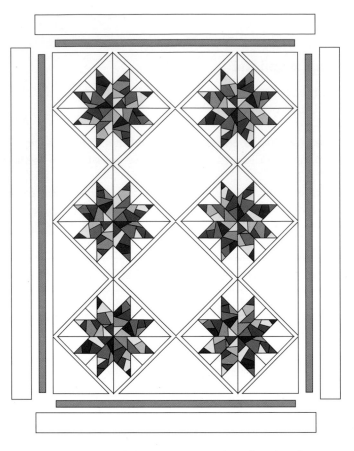

The inner and outer borders have butted corners. If there are more than four border strips, piece the strips end to end to make one long strip.

For all the settings, measure the quilt top down the center and cut the two inner border strips this length. Sew the border strips to the sides. Measure across the width, including the borders, and cut the two inner border strips this length. Sew these to the top and bottom.

Measure the quilt top down the center and cut the two outer border strips this length. Sew the strips to the sides. Measure across the width, including the borders, and cut the two strips this length. Sew these to the top and bottom.

Finishing the Quilt

See Part Four for suggestions on quilting design and binding. To determine the size of the backing, measure the quilt top in both directions and add 4" to each measurement. Sew panels together if needed. Use your favorite methods for layering, quilting, and binding.

Stars a la Carte – Bethany S. Reynolds

NURSERY STARS by author, 1998. Free-motion quilting in the background adds textural interest to this simple quilt.

Checkerboard Quilt Plans with Six Stars

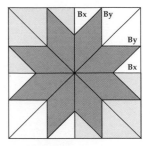

NURSERY STARS

See page 39
Skill Level with Basic Star Blocks: Easy
Finished Quilt with 6" Blocks (shown): 27" x 36"
Finished Quilt with 12" Blocks: 54" x 72"

Fabric Requirements (Measurements in yards unless otherwise indicated)		
	6" Blocks	**12" Blocks**
Background Fabrics B1 and B2	½ each of 2	1⅜ each of 2
One Color Star Blocks Diamonds*	⅛ each of 6	⅛ each of 6
Border Fabric	⅝ (seamless)	1⅜ (pieced) or 1⅞ (seamless)
Binding	⅜	¾
Backing	1	3½
*To substitute a different block, refer to the Star Fabric Yardage Charts on page 85.		

Star Blocks

Cut the diamond units for the one-color star blocks (or prepare the diamonds for the substitute block of your choice), following the directions in Part One.

Cutting Background Fabric for Star Blocks			
Block Size	**From *each* Fabric (B1 and B2), First Cut**	**Second Cut**	**Cut *each* square once on the diagonal to make...**
6"	(1) 2⅛" strip across width	(12) 2⅛" squares	(24) **Bx** triangles of *each* fabric
	(1) 2⅝" strip across width	(12) 2⅝" squares	(24) **By** triangles of *each* fabric
12"	(1) 3⅜" strip across width	(12) 3⅜" squares	(24) **Bx** triangles of *each* fabric
	(2) 4⅜" strips across width	(12) 4⅜" squares	(24) **By** triangles of *each* fabric

Piece six star blocks, using the Checkerboard Variation.

Preparing the Checkerboard Sashing

Following the chart, cut strips from the two background fabrics. Sew the strips together in pairs, one of each color, and cut the strips into segments to make the rectangular sashing units.

Cutting and Piecing the Checkerboard Sashing		
Block Size	**From Each Background Fabric, Cut**	**Piece strips in pairs and cut crosswise to make…**
6"	(2) 3½" strips across width	(23) 3½" x 6½" rectangle units
12"	(4) 6½" strips across width	(23) 6½" x 12½" rectangle units

Arrange the star and sashing units, following the Quilt Assembly Diagram. Rotate the units as needed to create the checkerboard effect. Take apart two of the rectangle units. Use these separate squares to complete the horizontal sashing rows. Sew the vertical seams in each row, then sew the horizontal rows together.

Adding the Outer Border

Cutting Outer Borders	
Block Size	**Cut**
6"	(4) 3½" strips across width
12"	(6) 6½" strips across width or (4) 6½" x 62" strips cut lengthwise

The borders have butted corners. If there are more than four border strips, piece the strips end to end to make one long strip. Measure the quilt top down the center and cut two strips this length. Sew the border strips to the sides. Measure across the width, including the straight border, and cut two strips this length. Sew these to the top and bottom.

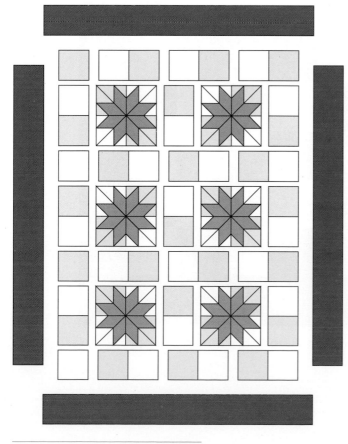

Finishing the Quilt

See Part Four for suggestions on quilting design and binding. To determine the size of the backing, measure the quilt top in both directions and add 4" to each measurement. Sew panels together if needed. Use your favorite methods for layering, quilting, and binding.

Color Key
☐ Background Fabric 1
☐ Background Fabric 2
■ Border Accent Fabric
■ Star Fabric

VIEWER ADVISORY: CONTAINS GRAPHIC MATERIALS by author, 1999. Stars in a bold marble print are cut using the Stack-n-Whack™ method for extra impact.

Checkerboard Quilt Plans with Twelve Stars

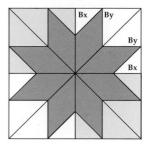

VIEWER ADVISORY: CONTAINS GRAPHIC MATERIALS

Skill Level with Basic Star Blocks: Easy
Finished Quilt with 6" Blocks: 36" x 45"
Finished Quilt with 12" Blocks (shown): 72" x 90"

Fabric Requirements		
(Measurements in yards unless otherwise indicated)		
	6" Blocks	**12" Blocks**
Background Fabrics B1 and B2	⅞ each of 2	2 each of 2
One Color Star Blocks Diamonds*	½	1¼
Border Fabric	⅝ (seamless)	1⅝ (pieced) or 2⅜ (seamless)
Binding	⅜	¾
Backing	1½	5½

*These yardages are for basic one color stars. For the Stack-n-Whack™ version shown in the sample, see the yardage and cutting information on page 21. To substitute another star block, use the Star Fabric Yardage Charts on page 85.

Star Blocks

Cut the diamond units for the one-color star blocks (or prepare the diamonds for the substitute block of your choice), following the directions in Part One.

Cutting Background Fabric for Star Blocks			
Block Size	**From *each* Fabric (B1 and B2), First Cut**	**Second Cut**	**Cut *each* square once on the diagonal to make...**
6"	(2) 2⅛" strip across width	(24) 2⅛" squares	(48) **Bx** triangles of *each* fabric
	(2) 2⅝" strip across width	(24) 2⅝" squares	(48) **By** triangles of *each* fabric
12"	(2) 3⅜" strip across width	(24) 3⅜" squares	(48) **Bx** triangles of *each* fabric
	(3) 4⅜" strips across width	(24) 4⅜" squares	(48) **By** triangles of *each* fabric

Piece 12 star blocks, using the Checkerboard Variation.

Preparing the Checkerboard Sashing

Following the chart below, cut strips from the two background fabrics. Sew the strips together in pairs, one of each color, and cut the strips into segments to make the rectangular sashing units.

Quilt Plans

Cutting and Piecing the Checkerboard Sashing		
Block Size	From *each* Background Fabric, cut	Piece strips in pairs and cut crosswise to make...
6"	(4) 3½" strips across width	(41) 3½" x 6½" rectangle units
12"	(7) 6½" strips across width	(41) 6½" x 12½" rectangle units

Arrange the star and sashing units, following the Quilt Assembly Diagram. Rotate the units as needed to create the checkerboard effect.

Sew the vertical seams in each row, then sew the horizontal rows together.

Adding the Outer Border

Cutting Outer Borders	
Block Size	Cut
6"	(4) 3½" strips across width or (4) 3½" strips x 41" strips cut lengthwise
12"	(8) 6½" strips across width or (4) 6½" x 80" strips cut lengthwise

The borders have butted corners. If there are more than four border strips, piece the strips end to end to make one long strip.

Measure the quilt top down the center and cut two strips this length. Sew the border strips to the sides. Measure across the width, including the straight border, and cut two strips this length. Sew these to the top and bottom.

Finishing the Quilt

See Part Four for suggestions on quilting design and binding. To determine the size of the backing, measure the quilt top in both directions and add 4" to each measurement. Sew panels together if needed. Use your favorite methods for layering, quilting, and binding.

TURN OF A DIFFERENT CENTURY by author, 1998. Subtle background fabrics enhance the reproduction fabric stars. The diagonal straight-line quilting frames the stars and creates the illusion of an on-point setting.

Night and Noon Quilt Plans with Twelve Stars

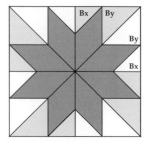

TURN OF A DIFFERENT CENTURY

See page 45
Skill Level with Basic Star Blocks: Easy
Finished Quilt with 6" Blocks (shown): 42" x 42"
Finished Quilt with 12" Blocks: 84" x 84"

Fabric Requirements		
(Measurements in yards unless otherwise indicated)		
	6" Blocks	**12" Blocks**
Background Fabrics B1 (center blocks only)	1¼	2½
Background Fabrics B2 (center and border blocks)	1⅝	4
Border Accent Fabric	½	1¼
Scrap Star Blocks Diamonds*: scraps totaling at least…	⅞	1⅜
Binding	½	¾
Backing	2¾	7½
*To substitute a different block, see the Star Fabric Yardage Charts on page 85.		

Star Blocks

Cut the diamond units for the Scrap Star Blocks (or prepare the diamonds for the substitute block of your choice), following the directions in Part One.

Cutting Background Fabric for Star Blocks			
Block Size	**From *each* Fabric (B1 and B2), First Cut**	**Second Cut**	**Cut *each* square once on the diagonal to make…**
6"	(2) 2⅛" strip across width	(24) 2⅛" squares	(48) **Bx** triangles of *each* fabric
	(2) 2⅝" strip across width	(24) 2⅝" squares	(48) **By** triangles of *each* fabric
12"	(2) 3⅜" strip across width	(24) 3⅜" squares	(48) **Bx** triangles of *each* fabric
	(3) 4⅜" strips across width	(24) 4⅜" squares	(48) **By** triangles of *each* fabric

Piece 12 star blocks, using the Night and Noon Variation.

Piecing the Alternate Pinwheel Blocks and Border Blocks

Make pieced squares from the background and border fabrics, using the grid method (see General Instructions, page 97), as follows:

Make four 3 x 4 square grids of B1 and B2 to make 96 pieced squares. Make two 3 x 4 square grids and one 1 x 2 square grid of B2 and the accent fabric to make 52 pieced squares for the "border."

6" Block Quilt Plans: Use a 4" grid and trim the pieced squares to 3½".
12" Block Quilt Plans: Use a 7" grid and trim the pieced squares to 6½".

Use these pieced squares to make the alternate pinwheel blocks and border blocks, following the illustrated instructions.

Night and Noon Setting Units

Make these pieced half-square triangle units by using the grid method or your preferred method. The trimmed units should measure 3½" square (3" finished size) for the 6" Block Quilt Plans, or 6½" square (6" finished size) for the 12" Block Quilt Plans.

Background **B1**/Background **B2**
Pieced Squares
Make 96

Background **B2**/Border Fabric
Pieced Squares
Make 52

Use the pieced half-square triangle units to make the setting blocks. These should measure 6½" for the 6" Block Quilt Plans, or 12½" for the 12" Block Quilt Plans.

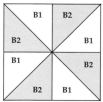

Pinwheel Alternate
Block
Make 13

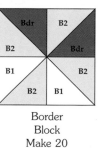

Border
Block
Make 20

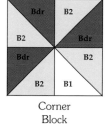

Corner
Block
Make 4

Color Key
☐ Background Fabric 1
☐ Background Fabric 2
■ Border Accent Fabric
■ Star Fabric

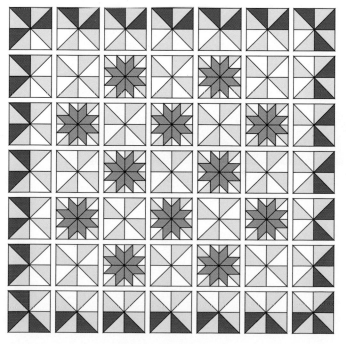

Assembling the Quilt

Arrange the star and setting blocks, following the Quilt Assembly Diagram. Sew the vertical seams in each row, then sew the horizontal rows together.

Finishing the Quilt

See Part Four for suggestions on quilting design and binding. To determine the size of the backing, measure the quilt top in both directions and add 4" to each measurement. Sew panels together if needed. Use your favorite methods for layering, quilting, and binding.

MIXED GREENS by author, 1999. The Stargazer setting makes an effective frame for these bright Compass Stars.

Stargazer Quilt Plan with Five Stars

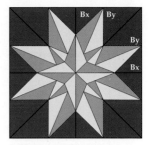

MIXED GREENS

Skill Level with Basic Star Blocks: Intermediate
Finished Quilt with 6" Blocks (shown): 30" x 30"
Finished Quilt with 12" Blocks: 60" x 60"

Fabric Requirements (Measurements in yards unless otherwise indicated)		
	6" Blocks	**12" Blocks**
Background Fabric	1	2⅛
Compass Star* Blocks Diamonds	⅜ each of 2	¾ each of 2
Accent Fabric for Stargazer Blocks	½	1
Border Fabric	¾	1⅜
Binding	⅜	½
Backing	1	3¾
*To substitute a different block, see the Star Fabric Yardage Charts on page 85.		

Star Blocks

Prepare diamond units for five Compass Star blocks (pages 28–31), or the substitute star block of your choice, following the cutting and piecing instructions in Part One.

Cutting Background Fabric for Star Blocks			
Block Size	**First Cut**	**Second Cut**	**Cut *each* square once on the diagonal to make...**
6"	(2) 2⅛" strips across width	(20) 2⅛" squares	(40) **Bx** triangles
	(2) 2⅝" strips across width	(20) 2⅝" squares	(40) **By** triangles
12"	(2) 3⅜" strips across width	(20) 3⅜" squares	(40) **Bx** triangles
	(3) 4⅜" strips across width	(20) 4⅜" squares	(40) **By** triangles

Cut the background fabric for the star blocks.

Piece five star blocks.

Cutting the Stargazer Block Fabrics

Cut 45° triangle wedges and corner triangles for the Stargazer blocks, following the illustrated instructions. The 45° Triangle Cutting Guides are on pages 51–52.

Quilt Plans

Cutting 45° Triangle Wedges			
Block Size	**Fabric**	**First Cut**	**Second Cut**
6"	Background	(4) 4" strips across width	(72) 45° triangle wedges (20 per strip)
	Accent	(2) 4" strips across width	(32) 45° triangle wedges (20 per strip)
	Border	(3) 4" strips across width	(56) 45° triangle wedges (20 per strip)
12"	Background	(6) 7" strips across width	(72) 45° triangle wedges (12 per strip)
	Accent	(3) 7" strips across width	(32) 45° triangle wedges (12 per strip)
	Border	(5) 7" strips across width	(56) 45° triangle wedges (12 per strip)

Cutting Corner Triangles				
Block Size	**Fabric**	**First Cut**	**Second Cut**	**Cut *each* square once on the diagonal to make...**
6"	Background	(1) 2⅝" strip across width	(6) 2⅝" squares	(12) corner triangles
	Accent	(2) 2⅝" strips across width	(16) 2⅝" squares	(32) corner triangles
	Border	(2) 2⅝" strips across width	(18) 2⅝" squares	(36) corner triangles
12"	Background	(1) 4⅜" strip across width	(6) 4⅜" squares	(12) corner triangles
	Accent	(2) 4⅜" strips across width	(16) 4⅜" squares	(32) corner triangles
	Border	(2) 4⅜" strips across width	(18) 4⅜" squares	(36) corner triangles

Piecing the Stargazer Blocks

Following the illustrated block piecing instructions, piece the alternate blocks and border blocks needed for your layout.

Assembling the Quilt

Arrange the Star and Stargazer blocks, following the Quilt Assembly Diagram, page 53. Sew the vertical seams in each row, then sew the horizontal rows together.

Finishing the Quilt

See Part Four for suggestions on quilting design and binding. To determine the size of the backing, measure the quilt top in both directions and add 4" to each measurement. Sew panels together if needed. Use your favorite methods for layering, quilting, and binding.

Cutting 45° Triangle Wedges

This wedge-shaped triangle has two equal sides, a 45° angle at the narrowest point, and 67.5° angles at the other two points. The straight grain should run through the center of the triangle. The cutting angle for this triangle is an odd one you won't find on a standard rotary ruler, so we've provided a Cutting Guide for these projects (page 52).*

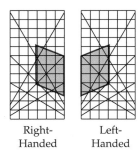

Right-
Handed   Left-
Handed

Prepare the Cutting Guide for the block size you're using in one of two ways:

• Trace the guide accurately on clear template plastic. Cut the guide out on the line. With clear tape, attach the plastic guide to the underside of your ruler, with the right edge of the ruler on the right edge of the guide, OR...

• Lay your ruler over the Cutting Guide with the right edge of the ruler on the right edge of the guide. Mark the guide lines on the ruler with a permanent marker or tape.

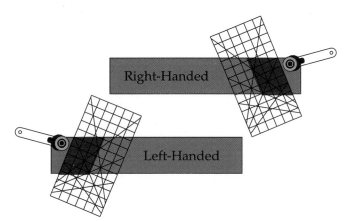

Right-Handed

Left-Handed

Fold your fabric with selvages together. Cut a strip across the width of the fabric, using the strip width given for the size block you are making. The illustrations show the 4" strip used for 6" blocks. You can cut several strips and stack them neatly for the next step.

---

*Note

The Stack-n-Whack™ 45° Cutting Guide may also be used to cut these wedges (see Sources, page 127).

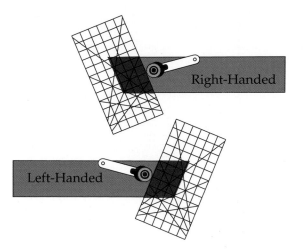

Right-Handed

Left-Handed

Lay the ruler with the Cutting Guide down on the stacked strips with the top and bottom edges of the guide aligned with the edges of the strips. Place the edge of the ruler far enough in to avoid the selvages. Cut along the edge through all layers. Set aside this first cut–this is scrap fabric.

Carefully turn the strips around so the angled edge is to your left (or to your right if you're left-handed). Lay the ruler down with the left edge of the Cutting Guide on the angled edge and cut.

Right-Handed   Left-Handed

Align the 45° line of your ruler with the cut edge of the piece and cut from point to point to make two sets of 45° triangle wedges. Set these aside. Continue cutting wedges from the strip.

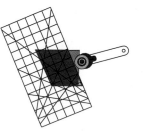

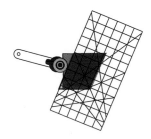

Right-Handed   Left-Handed

Continue cutting additional strips until you have the number of wedges required for your project.

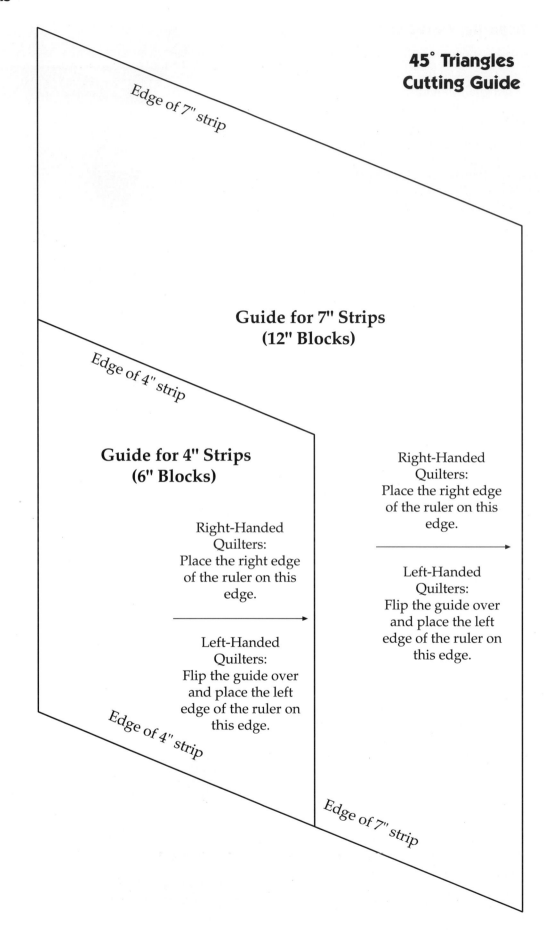

**45° Triangles
Cutting Guide**

Edge of 7" strip

**Guide for 7" Strips
(12" Blocks)**

Edge of 4" strip

**Guide for 4" Strips
(6" Blocks)**

Right-Handed
Quilters:
Place the right edge
of the ruler on this
edge.

Right-Handed
Quilters:
Place the right edge
of the ruler on this
edge.

Left-Handed
Quilters:
Flip the guide over
and place the left
edge of the ruler on
this edge.

Left-Handed
Quilters:
Flip the guide over
and place the left
edge of the ruler on
this edge.

Edge of 4" strip

Edge of 7" strip

Piecing the Stargazer Blocks

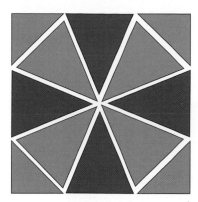

Each block has eight wedges and four corner triangles. Follow the block diagrams and the color key to lay out the correct fabric combinations for each block.

Make pairs of triangles by sewing from the outer edge to the block center with a ¼" seam allowance. Press the seam allowances open.

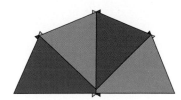

Place two pairs together and stitch from the outer edge to the center. Repeat with the other two pairs. Clip the triangle tips from the seam allowances and press the allowances open.

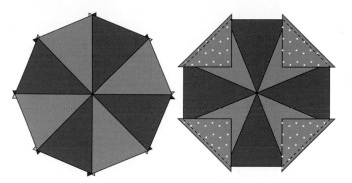

Place the halves right sides together and stitch across the center of the block, matching the crossed seams at the center of the block. Clip the triangle tips at the center. Press this seam allowance open.

Add corner triangles to four sides, centering the corner triangles on the wedges. Press the seam allowances toward the corner triangles.

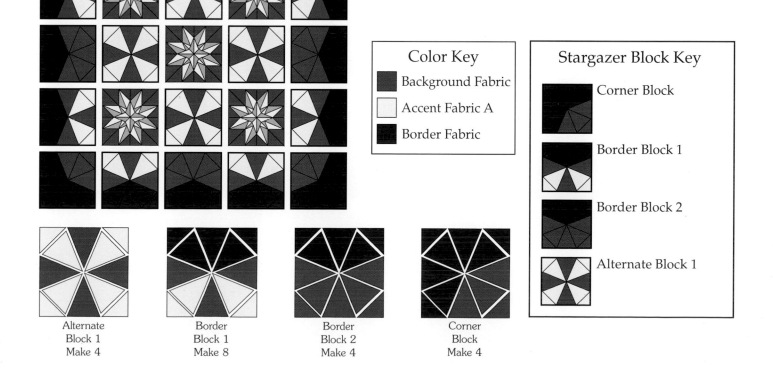

Color Key

- ■ Background Fabric
- □ Accent Fabric A
- ■ Border Fabric

Stargazer Block Key

- Corner Block
- Border Block 1
- Border Block 2
- Alternate Block 1

Alternate Block 1 Make 4

Border Block 1 Make 8

Border Block 2 Make 4

Corner Block Make 4

MILKY WAY by author, 1998. A dozen Split Stars form constellations in a twinkling night sky.

Stargazer Quilt Plans with Twelve Stars

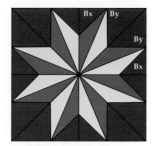

Milky Way & Summer Solstice

Skill Level with Basic Star Blocks: Intermediate
Finished Quilt with 6" Blocks (shown on page 54): 42" x 42"
Finished Quilt with 12" Blocks (shown on page 22): 84" x 84"

Fabric Requirements (Measurements in yards unless otherwise indicated)		
	6" Blocks	**12" Blocks**
Background Fabric	1¾	4¼
Split Star* Blocks Diamonds	⅝ each of 2	1⅜ each of 2
Accent Fabric for Stargazer Blocks	⅞	1⅞
Border Fabric	¾	2
Binding	⅜	¾
Backing	2¾	7½

*For the Stack-n-Whack™ version shown in SUMMER SOLSTICE, page 22, see the yardage and cutting information on page 21. To substitute another star block, use the Star Fabric Yardage Charts on page 85.

Star Blocks

Prepare diamond units for 12 Split Star blocks (pages 26–27) or substitute the star block of your choice, following the cutting and piecing instructions in Part One.

Cut the background fabric for the star blocks.

Cutting Background Fabric for Star Blocks			
Block Size	**First Cut**	**Second Cut**	**Cut *each* square once on the diagonal to make...**
6"	(3) 2⅛" strips across width	(48) 2⅛" squares	(96) **Bx** triangles
	(3) 2⅝" strips across width	(48) 2⅝" squares	(96) **By** triangles
12"	(4) 3⅜" strips across width	(48) 3⅜" squares	(96) **Bx** triangles
	(6) 4⅜" strips across width	(48) 4⅜" squares	(96) **By** triangles

Piece 12 star blocks.

Cutting the Stargazer Block Fabrics

Cut 45° triangle wedges and corner triangles for the Stargazer blocks, following the illustrated instructions. The 45° Triangle Cutting Guides are on pages 51–52.

Quilt Plans

Cutting 45° Triangle Wedges			
Block Size	**Fabric**	**First Cut**	**Second Cut**
6"	Background	(8) 4" strips across width	(152) 45° triangle wedges (20 per strip)
	Accent	(4) 4" strips across width	(64) 45° triangle wedges (20 per strip)
	Border	(4) 4" strips across width	(80) 45° triangle wedges (20 per strip)
12"	Background	(13) 7" strips across width	(152) 45° triangle wedges (12 per strip)
	Accent	(6) 7" strips across width	(64) 45° triangle wedges (12 per strip)
	Border	(7) 7" strips across width	(80) 45° triangle wedges (12 per strip)

Cutting Corner Triangles				
Block Size	**Fabric**	**First Cut**	**Second Cut**	**Cut *each* square once on the diagonal to make...**
6"	Background	(1) 2⅝" strips across width	(16) 2⅝" squares	(32) corner triangles
	Accent	(2) 2⅝" strips across width	(32) 2⅝" squares	(64) corner triangles
	Border	(2) 2⅝" strips across width	(27) 2⅝" squares	(52) corner triangles
12"	Background	(2) 4⅜" strips across width	(16) 4⅜" squares	(32) corner triangles
	Accent	(4) 4⅜" strips across width	(32) 4⅜" squares	(64) corner triangles
	Border	(3) 4⅜" strips across width	(27) 4⅜" squares	(52) corner triangles

Piecing the Stargazer Blocks

Following the illustrated block piecing instructions on page 53, piece the alternate blocks and border blocks needed for your layout.

Assembling the Quilt

Arrange the Star and Stargazer blocks, following the Quilt Assembly Diagram. Sew the vertical seams in each row, then sew the horizontal rows together.

Finishing the Quilt

See Part Four for suggestions on quilting design and binding. To determine the size of the backing, measure the quilt top in both directions and add 4" to each measurement. Sew panels together if needed. Use your favorite methods for layering, quilting, and binding.

Alternate
Block 1
Make 9

Alternate
Block 2
Make 4

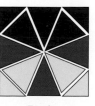

Border
Block 1
Make 8

Border
Block 2
Make 12

Corner
Block
Make 4

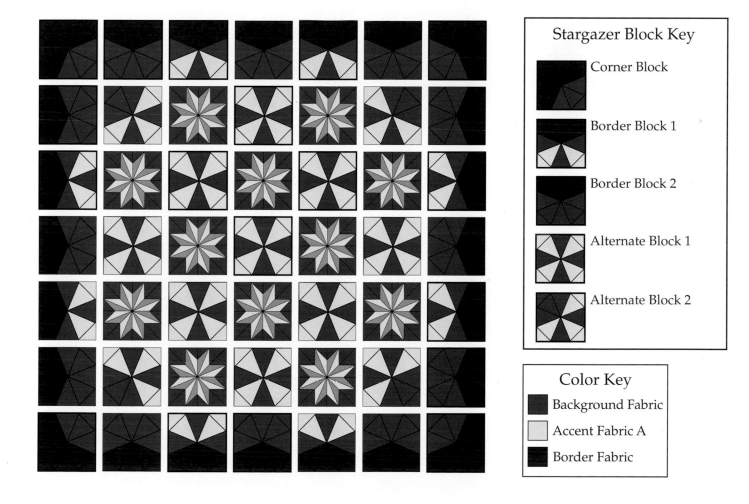

Stargazer Block Key

Corner Block

Border Block 1

Border Block 2

Alternate Block 1

Alternate Block 2

Color Key

Background Fabric

Accent Fabric A

Border Fabric

NIGHT FLIGHT by author, 1999. An aboriginal print from Australia created dramatic Stack-n-Whack™ stars.

Stars a la Carte – Bethany S. Reynolds

Swallowtail Quilt Plans with Eight Stars

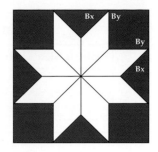

NIGHT FLIGHT

Skill Level with Basic Star Blocks: Advanced Intermediate
Finished Quilt with 6" Blocks: 27" x 39"
Finished Quilt with 12" Blocks (shown): 54" x 78"

Fabric Requirements (Measurements in yards unless otherwise indicated)		
	6" Blocks	**12" Blocks**
Background	1⅝	3¾
Star Diamond Fabric*	½	⅞
Accent Fabrics A and C – Swallowtail Blocks and Border	½ each of 2	¾ each of 2
Outer Border	⅜ (seamless)	⅞ (pieced) or 2¼ (seamless)
Binding	⅜	⅝
Backing	1	3½

*These yardages are for basic one color stars. For the Stack-n-Whack™ version shown in the sample, see the yardage and cutting information on page 21. To substitute another star block, us the Star Fabric Yardage Charts on page 85.

Star Blocks, Swallowtail Blocks, and Border Units

Cut diamonds for eight one-color star blocks (page 10–11), or prepare the diamonds for the substitute star block of your choice, following the cutting and piecing instructions in Part One.

Cutting Background Fabric Triangles for Swallowtail Quilt Plans			
Block Size	**First Cut**	**Second Cut**	**Cut *each* square once on the diagonal to make...**
6"	(7) 2⅛" strips across width	(96) 2⅛" squares	(192) **Bx** triangles
	(2) 2⅝" strips across width	(32) 2⅝" squares	(64) **By** triangles
12"	(8) 3⅜" strips across width	(96) 3⅜" squares	(192) **Bx** triangles
	(4) 4⅜" strips across width	(32) 4⅜" squares	(64) **By** triangles

Cut the background fabric for the star blocks, Swallowtail blocks, and border units.

Piece eight star blocks of your choice, following the instructions in Part One. Save the remaining Bx triangles for the Swallowtail blocks and border blocks.

Quilt Plans

Cutting Background Fabric Squares for Swallowtail Quilt Plans		
Block Size	**First Cut**	**Second Cut**
6"	(7) 3⅞" strips across width	(64) 3⅞" squares
12"	(11) 6⅞" strips across width	(64) 6⅞" squares

Pre-Cutting Accent Fabrics for Swallowtail Quilt Plans		
Block Size	**First Cut**	**Second Cut**
6"	(8) 1⅜" strips across width from *each* fabric (**A** and **C**)	(64) 1⅜" x 4½" rectangles of *each* fabric
12"	(13) 2" strips across width from *each* fabric (**A** and **C**)	(64) 2" x 7½" rectangles of *each* fabric

Piece seven Swallowtail blocks, following the instructions.

Paper Piecing the Swallowtail Block

Color Key	
■	Background Fabric
□	Accent Fabric A
▨	Accent Fabric B and Outer Border

Quarter-Blocks

You will need 64 quarter-block units. Twenty-eight of these units will be used for the seven setting blocks, and the remaining 36 units will be used for the border. Make 16 copies of the small foundations on page 116 or 64 copies of the large foundation on page 115, depending on the size block you want to make.

Set the stitch length on your sewing machine to a shorter than normal setting. Center a square of background fabric (B) under the foundation, with the wrong side of the fabric facing the unprinted side of the foundation. Hold in place with a pin or a dab of glue stick.

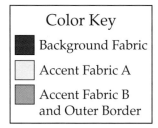

Fold the foundation back along the seam line between areas #1 and #2. Trim the excess background fabric to ¼" from the seam line.

Place a rectangle of Fabric A under the background fabric, with right sides together. Line up the edge of the rectangle with the trimmed edge of the background fabric, and center the seam line along the length of the rectangle.

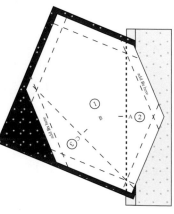

Fold the foundation back out flat. Stitch along the line, beginning and ending at the outer cutting lines.

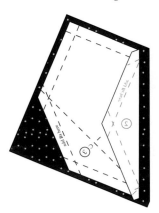

Press the Fabric A rectangle over the foundation.

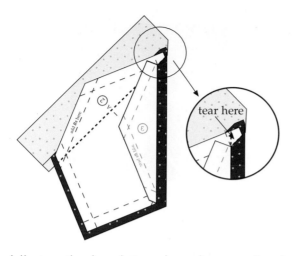

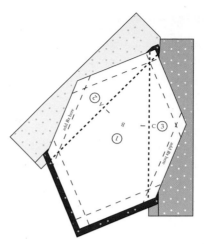

Carefully tear the foundation along the seam line in the seam allowance, as shown in the detail. Fold the foundation back along the seam line between areas #1 and #3. Trim the excess background fabric to ¼" from the seam line.

Press the Fabric C rectangle over the foundation (back and front views).

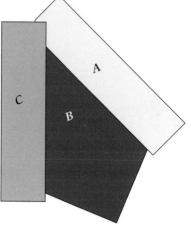

Place a rectangle of Fabric C under the background fabric, with right sides together. Place the right edge of the rectangle along the trimmed edge, and center the seam line along the length of the rectangle.

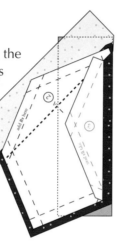

Trim along the outer cutting lines to complete the paper pieced unit.

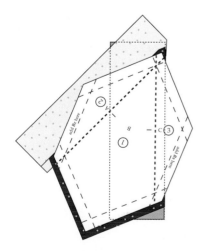

Fold the foundation back into place. Stitch along the line, beginning and ending at the outer cutting lines.

Quilt Plans

Completing the Quarter-Block Units

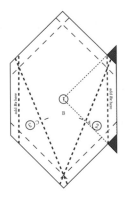

Sew the Bx triangles to the foundation where indicated, as follows: Place a Bx triangle, right sides together, under the foundation. Align the raw edges and center the long edge of the Bx triangle on the seam line so that the tips extend the same amount. Sew the triangle to the foundation.

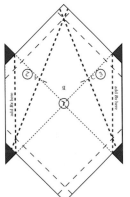

Add a Bx triangle to the opposite edge of the foundation.

Press the background fabric triangles over to complete the quarter-block unit. Carefully remove the paper foundations.

Completing the Swallowtail Block

Sew pairs of quarter-block units together to make half-blocks, matching the seams.

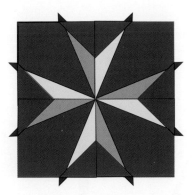

Sew half-blocks together to complete the block.

Piecing the Half-Block Border Units

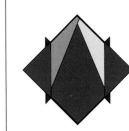

Reserve four quarter-block units for the corners.

Piece the remaining quarter-blocks together in pairs to make half-blocks.

Assembling the Quilt

Arrange the center and border blocks, following the Quilt Assembly Diagram. Sew the vertical seams in each row, then sew the horizontal rows together.

Stars a la Carte – Bethany S. Reynolds

Adding the Outer Borders

Cutting Outer Borders	
Block Size	**Cut**
6"	(4) 2" strips across width
12"	(7) 3½" strips across width or (4) 3½" x 74" strips cut lengthwise

The outer borders have butted corners. If there are more than four border strips, piece the strips end to end to make one long strip.

Measure the quilt top down the center and cut two strips this length. Sew the border strips to the sides. Measure across the width, including the straight border, and cut two strips this length. Sew these to the top and bottom.

Finishing the Quilt

See Part Four for suggestions on quilting design and binding. To determine the size of the backing, measure the quilt top in both directions and add 4" to each measurement. Sew panels together if needed. Use your favorite methods for layering, quilting, and binding.

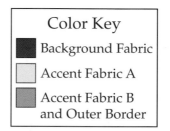

Color Key
Background Fabric
Accent Fabric A
Accent Fabric B and Outer Border

OUT FOR A SPIN by author, 1999. Hand-dyed fabrics and playful free-motion quilting give these Whirligig Stars a contemporary twist.

Diamond Border Quilt Plans with Five Stars

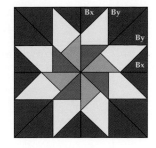

OUT FOR A SPIN

Skill Level with Basic Star Blocks: Easy
Finished Quilt with 6" Blocks: 27" x 27"
Finished Quilt with 12" Blocks (shown): 54" x 54"

Fabric Requirements (Measurements in yards unless otherwise indicated)		
	6" Blocks	**12" Blocks**
Background Fabric	1¼	3½
Whirligig Star Tips and Border Diamonds	⅝	1
Whirligig Star Whirligigs (C1 and C2)*	⅛ each of 2	¼ each of 2
Binding	⅜	½
Backing	1	3½
*To substitute different blocks or diamond borders, see pages 84–91.		

Star Blocks and Diamond Border Units

Prepare diamond units for five Whirligig Star blocks (pages 23–25) or substitute the star block of your choice, following the cutting and piecing instructions in Part One.

Cut the background fabric for the star block and diamond border units.

Cutting Background Fabric for Star Blocks and Diamond Border			
Block Size	**First Cut**	**Second Cut**	**Cut *each* square once on the diagonal to make…**
6"	(2) 2⅛" strips across width	(36) 2⅛" squares	(72) **Bx** triangles
	(3) 2⅝" strips across width	(36) 2⅝" squares	(72) **By** triangles
	(2) 3⅞" strips across width	(12) 3⅞" squares	(24) **Bz** triangles
12"	(3) 3⅜" strips across width	(36) 3⅜" squares	(72) **Bx** triangles
	(5) 4⅜" strips across width	(36) 4⅜" squares	(72) **By** triangles
	(2) 6⅞" strips across width	(12) 6⅞" squares	(24) **Bz** triangles

Piece the five star blocks, following the Star Block Piecing instructions in Part One (pages 12–14).

Quilt Plans

Cutting Star Fabric for One-Color Diamond Border Units*		
Block Size	First Cut	Second Cut
6"	(3) 1¾" strips across width	(32) 1¾" diamonds
12"	(4) 3" strips across width	(32) 3" diamonds
*Note: If you are substituting a different diamond unit for the border, follow the instructions in the Customizing the Diamond Border Quilt Plans section (page 89).		

Piece 16 left and 16 right diamond units for the border, following the Star Block Piecing instructions in Part One (pages 12–14). Do not piece the quarter-blocks yet.

Assembling the Quilt

Using 4 left and 4 right diamond units, piece 4 quarter-blocks. Set these quarter-blocks aside to use for the corners of the border.

To the remaining diamond units, add Bz triangles of background fabric. Piece these square units together in pairs.

Cutting Alternate Blocks and Outer Borders from Background Fabric		
Block Size	Borders – Cut	Plain Alternate Blocks – Cut
6"	(4) 2" strips across width	(4) 6½" squares
12"	(4) 3½" x 56" strips lengthwise	(4) 12½" squares from remaining fabric

Arrange the center and border blocks, following the Quilt Assembly Diagram. Sew the vertical seams in each row, then sew the horizontal rows together.

The outer borders have butted corners. Measure the quilt top down the center and cut two strips this length. Sew the border strips to the sides. Measure across the width, including the just-sewn border strips, and cut two strips this length. Sew these to the top and bottom.

Finishing the Quilt

See Part Four for suggestions on quilting design and binding. To determine the size of the backing, measure the quilt top in both directions and add 4" to each measurement. Sew panels together if needed. Use your favorite methods for layering, quilting, and binding.

One-Color Diamond Border Units

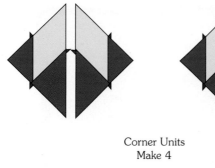

Corner Units
Make 4

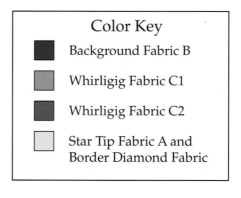

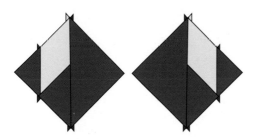

Left and Right
Quarter Blocks

Pieced Half-Block
Border Unit

Color Key

Background Fabric B

Whirligig Fabric C1

Whirligig Fabric C2

Star Tip Fabric A and
Border Diamond Fabric

YANKEE THRIFT by author, 1998. Friends helped test this pattern and contributed their blocks to this charming little quilt. The decorative red ties are a tribute to antique family quilts in the author's collection.

Diamond Border Quilt Plans with Six Stars

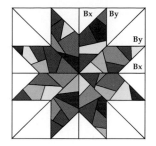

YANKEE THRIFT

Skill Level with Basic Star Blocks: Easy
Finished Quilt with 6" Blocks (shown): 21" x 27"
Finished Quilt with 12" Blocks: 42" x 54"

Fabric Requirements (Measurements in yards unless otherwise indicated)		
	6" Blocks	**12" Blocks**
Background Fabric: one fabric or assorted scraps totaling at least...	1	2¼ (pieced borders) or 3¼ (seamless borders)
Fabric for Crazy Eights Blocks and Border*: assorted scraps totaling at least...	¾	1⅜
Binding	⅜	½
Backing	¾	2¾
*To substitute different blocks or diamond borders, see pages 84–91.		

Star Blocks and Diamond Border Units

Prepare diamond units for six Crazy Eights blocks (pages 32–34) or the substitute star block of your choice, following the cutting and piecing instructions in Part One.

Cut the background fabric for the star block and diamond border units.

Cutting Background Fabric for Star Blocks and Diamond Border*			
Block Size	**First Cut**	**Second Cut**	**Cut *each* square once on the diagonal to make...**
6"	(2) 2⅛" strips across width	(38) 2⅛" squares	(76) **Bx** triangles
	(3) 2⅝" strips across width	(38) 2⅝" squares	(76) **By** triangles
	(1) 3⅞" strip across width	(10) 3⅞" squares	(20) **Bz** triangles
12"	(4) 3⅜" strips across width	(38) 3⅜" squares	(76) **Bx** triangles
	(5) 4⅜" strips across width	(38) 4⅜" squares	(76) **By** triangles
	(2) 6⅞" strips across width	(10) 6⅞" squares	(20) **Bz** triangles
*For a scrap style background, cut the required number of triangles from assorted fabrics.			

Quilt Plans

Piece the six star blocks, following the Star Block Piecing instructions in Part One (pages 12–14).

Prepare 28 Crazy Eights diamonds for the border. Note: If you are substituting a different diamond unit for the border, follow the instructions in the Customizing the Diamond Border Quilt Plans section (pages 89–91).

Piece 14 left and 14 right diamond units, following the Star Block Piecing instructions in Part One (pages 12–14). Do not piece the quarter-blocks yet.

Assembling the Quilt

Using 4 left and 4 right diamond units, piece 4 quarter-blocks. Set these quarter-blocks aside to use for the corners of the border.

To the remaining diamond units, add Bz triangles of background fabric. Piece these square units together in pairs.

Arrange the center and border blocks, following the Quilt Assembly Diagram. Sew the vertical seams in each row, then sew the horizontal rows together.

Cutting Outer Borders from Background Fabric	
Block Size	**Cut**
6"	(4) 2" strips across width
12"	(5) 3½" strips across width or (4) 3½" x 50" strips cut lengthwise

The outer borders have butted corners. If there are more than four border strips, piece the strips end to end to make one long strip.

Measure the quilt top down the center and cut two strips this length. Sew the border strips to the sides. Measure across the width, including the just sewn border strips, and cut two strips this length. Sew these to the top and bottom.

Finishing the Quilt

See Part Four for suggestions on quilting design and binding. To determine the size of the backing, measure the quilt top in both directions and add 4" to each measurement. Sew panels together if needed. Use your favorite methods for layering, quilting, and binding.

Crazy Eights Diamond Border Units

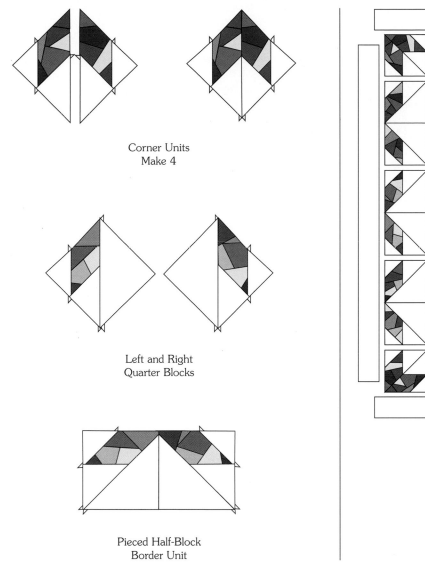

Corner Units
Make 4

Left and Right
Quarter Blocks

Pieced Half-Block
Border Unit

BIMINI BLUES by author, 1999. Watercolor prints in soft blues recall island breezes. The two-color border creates a twisting ribbon effect.

Stars a la Carte – Bethany S. Reynolds

Diamond Border Quilt Plans with Eight Stars

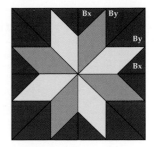

BIMINI BLUES

Skill Level with Basic Star Blocks: Easy
Finished Quilt with 6" Blocks (shown): 27" x 39"
Finished Quilt with 12" Blocks: 54" x 78"

Fabric Requirements		
(Measurements in yards unless otherwise indicated)		
	6" Blocks	**12" Blocks**
Background Fabric	1½	5¼
Two-Color Star Blocks and Border Diamonds*	⅜ each of 2	¾ each of 2
Binding	⅜	⅝
Backing	⅞	3¼
*To substitute different blocks or diamond borders, see pages 84–91.		

Star Blocks and Diamond Border Units

Cut diamonds for eight two-color star blocks (pages 10–11) or prepare the diamonds for the substitute star block of your choice, following the cutting and piecing instructions in Part One.

Cut the background fabric for the star block and diamond border units.

Cutting Background Fabric for Star Blocks and Diamond Border			
Block Size	**First Cut**	**Second Cut**	**Cut *each* square once on the diagonal to make...**
6"	(3) 2⅛" strips across width	(52) 2⅛" squares	(104) **Bx** triangles
	(4) 2⅝" strips across width	(52) 2⅝" squares	(104) **By** triangles
	(2) 3⅞" strips across width	(16) 3⅞" squares	(32) **Bz** triangles
12"	(5) 3⅜" strips across width	(52) 3⅜" squares	(104) **Bx** triangles
	(7) 4⅜" strips across width	(52) 4⅜" squares	(104) **By** triangles
	(3) 6⅞" strips across width	(16) 6⅞" squares	(32) **Bz** triangles

Piece the eight star blocks, following the Star Block Piecing instructions in Part One (pages 12–14).

Quilt Plans

Cutting Star Fabric for Two-Color Diamond Border Units*		
Block Size	**First Cut**	**Second Cut**
6"	(2) 1¾" strips across width from *each* fabric	(20) 1¾" diamonds from *each* fabric
12"	(3) 3" strips across width from *each* fabric	(20) 3" diamonds from *each* fabric
*Note: If you are substituting a different diamond unit for the border, follow the instructions in the "Customizing the Diamond Border Quilt Plans" section (pages 89–91).		

Piece 20 left and 20 right diamond units, following the Star Block Piecing instructions in Part One (pages 12–14). Do not piece the quarter-blocks yet.

Assembling the Quilt

Using 4 left and 4 right diamond units, piece 4 quarter-blocks. Set these quarter-blocks aside to use for the corners of the border.

To the remaining diamond units, add Bz triangles of background fabric. Piece these square units together in pairs.

Cutting Alternate Blocks and Outer Borders from Background Fabric		
Center Block Size	**Borders – Cut**	**Plain Alternate Blocks – Cut**
6"	(4) 2" strips across width	(7) 6½" squares
12"	(4) 3½" x 74" strips lengthwise	(7) 12½" squares from remaining fabric

Arrange the center and border blocks, following the Quilt Assembly Diagram. Sew the vertical seams in each row, then sew the horizontal rows together.

The outer borders have butted corners. Measure the quilt top down the center and cut two strips this length. Sew the border strips to the sides. Measure across the width, including the just sewn border strips, and cut two strips this length. Sew these to the top and bottom.

Finishing the Quilt

See Part Four for suggestions on quilting design and binding. To determine the size of the backing, measure the quilt top in both directions and add 4" to each measurement. Sew panels together if needed. Use your favorite methods for layering, quilting, and binding.

Two-Color Diamond Border Units

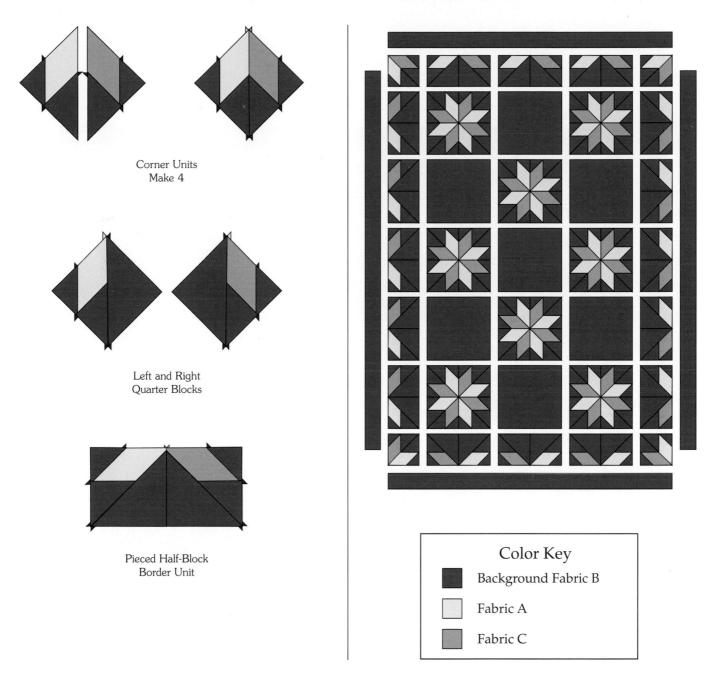

Corner Units
Make 4

Left and Right
Quarter Blocks

Pieced Half-Block
Border Unit

Color Key
■ Background Fabric B
□ Fabric A
■ Fabric C

CELESTIAL NAVIGATION by author, 1998. Compass Stars alternate with trapunto quilted wreaths in this large quilt.

Diamond Border Quilt Plans with Twelve Stars

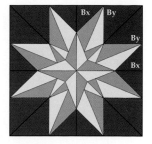

CELESTIAL NAVIGATION

Skill Level with Basic Star Blocks: Intermediate
Finished Quilt with 6" Blocks: 39" x 39"
Finished Quilt with 12" Blocks (shown): 78" x 78"

Fabric Requirements (Measurements in yards unless otherwise indicated)		
	6" Blocks	**12" Blocks**
Background Fabric	1⅞	5¼
Star Fabric: Compass Star Blocks and Split Diamond Border* – assorted scraps totaling at least...	1 each light (**A**) and dark (**C**)	2¼ each light (**A**) and dark (**C**)
Binding	½	¾
Backing	1¼	4¾
*To substitute different blocks or diamond borders, see pages 84–91.		

Star Blocks and Diamond Border Units

Prepare diamond units for 12 Compass Star blocks (pages 28–31) or the substitute the star block of your choice, following the cutting and piecing instructions in Part One.

Cut the background fabric for the star block and diamond border units.

Cutting Background Fabric for Star Blocks and Diamond Border				
Block Size	**First Cut**		**Second Cut**	**Cut *each* square once on the diagonal to make...**
6"	(4) 2⅛" strips across width		(72) 2⅛" squares	(144) **Bx** triangles
	(5) 2⅝" strips across width		(72) 2⅝" squares	(144) **By** triangles
	(2) 3⅞" strips across width		(20) 3⅞" squares	(24) **Bz** triangles
12"	(6) 3⅜" strips across width		(72) 3⅜" squares	(144) **Bx** triangles
	(9) 4⅜" strips across width		(72) 4⅜" squares	(144) **By** triangles
	(4) 6⅞" strips across width		(20) 6⅞" squares	(40) **Bz** triangles

Piece the 12 star blocks, following the Star Block Piecing instructions in Part One (pages 12–14).

Quilt Plans

Pre-Cutting Star Fabric for Split Diamond Border Units*		
Block Size	**From Each of Two Fabrics**, First Cut**	**Second Cut**
6"	(6) 1¼" strips across width or (2) 4¾" strips across width (lengthwise stripes)	(48) 1¼" x 4¾" rectangles from each fabric
12"	(10) 2" strips across width or (3) 8" strips across width (lengthwise stripes)	(48) 2" x 8" rectangles from each fabric
Note: If you are substituting a different diamond unit for the border, follow the instructions in the Customizing the Diamond Border Quilt Plans section (pages 89–91). ***For a scrap version, cut the required number of light and dark rectangles from assorted fabrics.*		

**For a scrap version, cut the required number of light and dark rectangles from assorted fabrics.

Prepare 48 Split Star border diamond (24 left and 24 right), following the illustrations on page 79. Use the foundations on page 117 or 118.

Piece 24 left and 24 right diamond units for the border, following the Star Block Piecing instructions in Part One (pages 12–14). Do not piece the quarter-blocks yet.

Assembling the Quilt

Using 4 left and 4 right diamond units, piece 4 quarter-blocks. Set these quarter-blocks aside to use for the corners of the border.

To the remaining diamond units, add Bz triangles of background fabric. Piece these square units together in pairs.

Cutting Alternate Blocks and Outer Borders from Background Fabric		
Center Block Size	**Borders – Cut**	**Plain Alternate Blocks – Cut**
6"	(4) 2" strips across width	(3) 6½" squares strips across width; cut into (13) 6½" squares
12"	(4) 3½" x 80" strips lengthwise	(13) 12½" squares from remaining fabric

Arrange the center and border blocks, following the Quilt Assembly Diagram. Sew the vertical seams in each row, then sew the horizontal rows together.

The outer borders have butted corners. Measure the quilt top down the center and cut two strips this length. Sew the border strips to the sides. Measure across the width, including the straight border, and cut two strips this length. Sew these to the top and bottom.

Finishing the Quilt

See Part Four for suggestions on quilting design and binding. To determine the size of the backing, measure the quilt top in both directions and add 4" to each measurement. Sew panels together if needed. Use your favorite methods for layering, quilting, and binding.

Stars a la Carte – Bethany S. Reynolds

Split Diamond Border

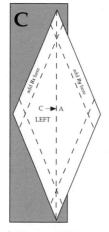

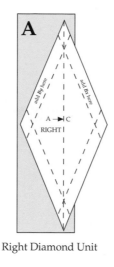

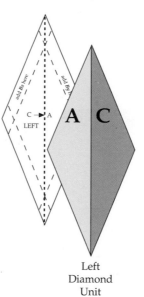

Left Diamond Unit

Right Diamond Unit

Left Diamond Unit

Right Diamond Unit

Split Diamond Border Units

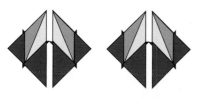

Corner Units
Make 4

Left and Right
Quarter Blocks

Pieced Half-Block
Border Unit

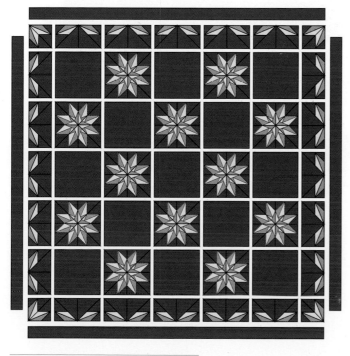

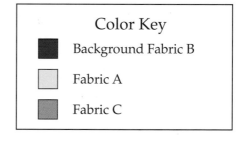

Color Key

■ Background Fabric B

□ Fabric A

▨ Fabric C

STRIPE IT RICH by author, 1999. Ethnic stripes from around the world come together in these Split Star blocks. Couched metallic floss and heavy rayon thread accent the stars and leaf appliqué.

Laurel Appliqué Quilt Plans with Five Stars

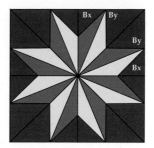

STRIPE IT RICH

Skill Level with Basic Star Blocks: Intermediate
Finished Quilt with 6" Blocks: 24" x 24"
Finished Quilt with 12" Blocks (shown): 48" x 48"

Fabric Requirements (Measurements in yards unless otherwise indicated)		
	6" Blocks	**12" Blocks**
Background Fabric	1	2½
Star Point Fabric (Split Star blocks*) – assorted stripes	scraps or ½ each of 10	scraps or ⅜ each of 10
Appliqué Fabric	⅝	1½
Optional: Paper-Backed Fusing Web (yardage based on 11" wide web; wider web may require less)	1	4
Binding	⅜	½
Backing	¾	3
*To substitute a different block, refer to the Star Fabric Yardage Charts on page 85.		

Star Blocks

Prepare diamond units for five Split Star blocks (pages 26–27) or the substitute star block of your choice, following the cutting and piecing instructions in Part One.

Cut the background fabric for the star blocks.

Cutting Background Fabric for Star Blocks			
Block Size	**First Cut**	**Second Cut**	**Cut *each* square once on the diagonal to make...**
6"	(2) 2⅛" strips across width	(20) 2⅛" squares	(40) **Bx** triangles
	(2) 2⅝" strips across width	(20) 2⅝" squares	(40) **By** triangles
12"	(2) 3⅜" strips across width	(20) 3⅜" squares	(40) **Bx** triangles
	(3) 4⅜" strips across width	(20) 4⅜" squares	(40) **By** triangles

Piece five star blocks, following the block piecing instructions in Part One.

Quilt Plans

Crossed Laurel Appliqué Blocks

Read through the general instructions for appliqué in Part Four (pages 99–100) before beginning.

Since the appliqué may draw in the fabric a bit, the blocks are cut slightly larger than needed. They should be trimmed after completing the appliqué, as noted in the instructions for assembling the quilt.

Cutting Background Fabric Squares for Appliqué Blocks		
Block Size	**First Cut**	**Second Cut**
6"	(1) 7" strip across width	(4) 7" squares
12"	(2) 13" strips across width	(4) 13" squares

Following the instructions on pages 99–100, prepare a total of 248 leaves for the blocks and border.

Appliqué the blocks using the method of your choice. Set aside the remaining leaves for the border. Add couching or other embroidery details to the blocks if desired.

Assembling the Quilt

Keeping the appliqué design centered, trim the completed appliqué blocks to 6½" for the small quilt or 12½" for the larger size. Arrange the center and border blocks, following the Quilt Assembly Diagram. Sew the vertical seams in each row, then sew the horizontal rows together.

Cutting the Border Strips from Background Fabric	
Center Block Size	**Cut**
6"	(4) 3½" x 20" strips across width and (4) 3½" cornerstone squares
12"	(4) 6½" x 38" strips cut lengthwise and (4) 6½" cornerstone squares

Adding the Appliqué Border

The borders are cut slightly longer than needed to allow for the take up for the appliqué. Press each side border in half lengthwise to mark the position for the stem. Fold each border with the short ends together to find the midpoint in the length, and mark this spot with removable marker or chalk. The leaf design will change direction at this midpoint on each side.

Begin placing the leaves at the midpoint on each border, and place them evenly along the stem line in the direction indicated in the illustrations. See the instructions for appliqué on pages 99–100 for tips on placing the leaves and completing the appliqué. Add the couched or embroidered stems and veins. To allow for adjustments in the length of the border, wait to appliqué and embroider the last one or two pairs of leaves at each end until the borders have been sewn in place.

Measure the quilt top down the center and cut two border strips to this length, trimming the excess evenly from each end so that the midpoint does not change. Measure across the width of the quilt top and cut two strips this length. Sew the side borders in place, matching the midpoint on each border to the midpoint on the quilt. Sew a cornerstone square (3½" square for the small quilt or 6½" square for the large one) to each end of the remaining two borders. Sew these borders to the top and bottom edges, matching the midpoints. Finish the appliqué and embroidery on the side borders at each corner, adjusting the placement of the leaves slightly if needed.

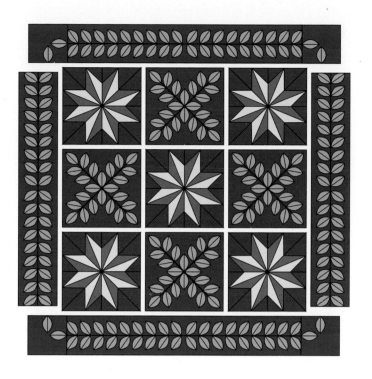

Finishing the Quilt

See Part Four for suggestions on quilting design and binding. To determine the size of the backing, measure the quilt top in both directions and add 4" to each measurement. Sew panels together if needed. Use your favorite methods for layering, quilting, and binding.

If desired, round off the corners of the quilt using the patterns on pages 121–122 before binding. Use bias-cut strips for the binding if you round off the corners.

The Quilt Plans in Part Two include the yardages for each setting with a specific star block. The charts in this section give separate yardage requirements for the star-point fabrics and the background fabric used in the star blocks. You can use these charts to help you plan your own variations.

- To substitute a different star block in a setting, use the Star Fabric Yardage Charts to determine any differences in the star fabric yardage that may be necessary. Since background fabric yardage for the star blocks is included in the Quilt Plans, you will not need to adjust the background yardage.

- If the sample is shown with the same fabric combination used for all the stars and you want to purchase various fabric combinations for the blocks, use the "1 Star" yardage figures in the Star Fabric Yardage Chart for each block. If the sample is shown with different fabric combinations and you prefer to use a single combination for all the stars, substitute the star fabric yardage figures for the number of stars needed.

- If you have not decided on a Quilt Plan and want to piece the star blocks first, use the Background Triangle Cutting Charts to cut the background fabric for the desired number of star blocks.

- If you want to use the Stack-n-Whack™ cutting method for the star blocks, refer to the yardage charts and instructions on pages 17–22.

- You might want to use one of the blocks in a setting of your own design. Use the Star Fabric Yardage Charts and the Background Fabric Yardage Charts to help plan your yardage requirements. Use the cutting charts in the star block chapter and the Background Triangle Cutting Charts in this chapter to easily determine the number of pieces needed for a given number of star blocks.

- The Diamond Border Quilt Plans feature interchangeable border choices. Use the charts beginning on page 90 to substitute a different diamond border for the one shown with a particular Quilt Plan.

Star Fabric Yardage Charts

Star Fabric Requirements – 6" Blocks (Measurements in yards unless otherwise indicated)					
	1 Star	**5 Stars**	**6 Stars**	**8 Stars**	**12 Stars**
One-Color Star	⅛	¼	⅜	⅜	½
Two-Color Star	⅛ each of 2	¼ each of 2	¼ each of 2	¼ each of 2	⅜ each of 2
Scrap Star or Crazy Eights: scraps totaling at least…	⅜	⅜	½	⅝	⅞
Whirligig Star					
Star Tip Fabric **A**	⅛	¼	¼	⅜	½
Whirligig Fabric **C**	⅛ each of 2	⅛ each of 2	⅛ each of 2	⅛ each of 2	¼ each of 2
Split Star Star	¼ each of 2	⅜ each of 2	⅜ each of 2	½ each of 2	⅝ each of 2
Compass Star	⅛ each of 2	⅜ each of 2	⅜ each of 2	⅝ each of 2	⅞ each of 2

Star Fabric Requirements – 12" Blocks (Measurements in yards unless otherwise indicated)					
	1 Star	**5 Stars**	**6 Stars**	**8 Stars**	**12 Stars**
One-Color Star	⅛	⅝	⅝	⅞	1¼
Two-Color Star	⅛ each of 2	⅜ each of 2	⅜ each of 2	½ each of 2	⅝ each of 2
Scrap Star or Crazy Eights: scraps totaling at least…	⅜	⅞	⅞	1⅛	1⅜
Whirligig Star					
Star Tip Fabric **A**	¼	½	½	¾	1
Whirligig Fabric **C**	¼ each of 2	¼ each of 2	⅜ each of 2	⅜ each of 2	½ each of 2
Split Star Star	⅜ each of 2	⅝ each of 2	¾ each of 2	1 each of 2	1⅛ each of 2
Compass Star	¼ each of 2	¾ each of 2	⅞ each of 2	1⅛ each of 2	1⅝ each of 2

Background Fabric Yardage Charts

Background fabric yardages are included in the Quilt Plans. These charts are for your reference if you want to design your own setting.

Star Block Background Fabric Requirements – 6" Blocks (Measurements in yards unless otherwise indicated)					
	1 Star	**5 Stars**	**6 Stars**	**8 Stars**	**12 Stars**
One-Color Background	⅛	⅜	⅜	½	⅝
Two-Color Background	¼ each of 2	¼ each of 2	¼ each of 2	⅜ each of 2	⅜ each of 2

Star Block Background Fabric Requirements – 12" Blocks (Measurements in yards unless otherwise indicated)					
	1 Star	**5 Stars**	**6 Stars**	**8 Stars**	**12 Stars**
One-Color Background	¼	¾	⅞	1	1⅜
Two-Color Background	⅜ each of 2	½ each of 2	½ each of 2	½ each of 2	¾ each of 2

Background Fabric Cutting Charts

The charts in this section give the background cutting figures for the basic Eight-Pointed Star block as well as the pieced diamond stars. One-color and two-color background versions are given. Use the two-color background charts for stars that will go in the Night and Noon or Checkerboard settings.

If you plan to make all the stars with the same background fabric, follow the cutting figures for the total number of stars needed. If each star will be different, use the single block cutting figures to cut the triangles for each block. For a scrap effect with a variety of background fabrics, refer to the One-Fabric Background chart to find the total number of Bx and By triangles for the number of stars desired.

Background Fabric Triangles for 6" Star Blocks – Single Fabric Background					
	1 Star	**5 Stars**	**6 Stars**	**8 Stars**	**12 Stars**
Cut this many 2⅛" strips across width:	1 (8½" long)	2	2	2	3
Cut strips into this many 2⅛" squares:	4	20	24	32	48
Cut each square once on the diagonal to make this many Bx triangles:	8	40	48	64	96
Cut this many 2⅝" strips across width:	1 (10½" long)	2	2	2	3
Cut strips into this many 2⅝" squares:	4	20	24	32	48
Cut each square once on the diagonal to make this many By triangles:	8	40	48	64	96

Background Fabric Triangles for 12" Star Blocks – Single Fabric Background					
	1 Star	**5 Stars**	**6 Stars**	**8 Stars**	**12 Stars**
Cut this many 3⅜" strips across width:	1 (13½" long)	2	2	3	4
Cut strips into this many 3⅜" squares:	4	20	24	32	48
Cut each square once on the diagonal to make this many Bx triangles:	8	40	48	64	96
Cut this many 4⅜" strips across width:	1 (17½" long)	3	3	4	6
Cut strips into this many 4⅜" squares:	4	20	24	32	48
Cut each square once on the diagonal to make this many By triangles:	8	40	48	64	96

Customizing Your Quilt

Background Fabric Triangles for 6" Star Blocks – Two Fabric Background

	1 Star	5 Stars	6 Stars	8 Stars	12 Stars
Cut this many 2⅛" strips across width from each fabric:	1 (4¼" long)	1	1	1	2
Cut strips into this many 2⅛" squares of each fabric:	2	10	12	16	24
Cut each square once on the diagonal to make this many Bx triangles or each fabric:	4	20	24	32	48
Cut this many 2⅝" strips across width from each fabric:	1 (5¼" long)	1	1	1	2
Cut strips into this many 2⅝" squares of each fabric:	2	10	12	16	24
Cut each square once on the diagonal to make this many By triangles or each fabric:	4	20	24	32	48

Background Fabric Triangles for 12" Star Blocks – Two Fabric Background

	1 Star	5 Stars	6 Stars	8 Stars	12 Stars
Cut this many 3⅜" strips across width from each fabric:	1 (6¾" long)	1	1	2	2
Cut strips into this many 3⅜" squares of each fabric:	2	10	12	16	24
Cut each square once on the diagonal to make this many Bx triangles or each fabric:	4	20	24	32	48
Cut this many 4⅜" strips across width from each fabric:	1 (8¾" long)	2	2	2	3
Cut strips into this many 4⅜" squares of each fabric:	2	10	12	16	24
Cut each square once on the diagonal to make this many By triangles or each fabric:	4	20	24	32	48

Customizing the Diamond Border Quilt Plans

The versatile settings in this category create dramatic frames for the center blocks. The simple Diamond Border in one or two colors suggests a twisting ribbon. The Split-Diamond Border nicely complements more intricate blocks like the Split Star and Compass Star. The Crazy Eights border is a perfect partner for the Crazy Eights blocks.

Any of the star blocks can be used in each of the quilt plans. The border designs are also interchangeable. To create your own combination of star blocks and diamond borders, choose the size quilt you want to make from the Diamond Border Quilt Plans. The background fabric yardage and cutting instructions given in the quilt plans will not change.

Use the yardage charts in this section and the star fabric yardage chart on page 85 to determine the yardage you'll need for the star and border accent fabrics. The cutting charts in this section give the cutting instructions for the border diamonds. Refer to the block chapters in Part One for the star block cutting charts.

For scrap versions of the one-color or Split Diamond Borders, disregard the directions for the number of strips needed. Simply cut the required strip width from scraps and cut the total number of pieces needed.

For paper pieced diamond borders, trace or photocopy the number of paper foundations listed. Piece the diamond units by following the instructions in the appropriate block chapter in Part One.

Illustrated piecing instructions for the border units are shown on the following pages:

One-Color Diamond Border, page 67

Two-Color Diamond Border, page 75

Split Star Diamond Border, page 79

Crazy Eights Diamond Border, page 71

Number of Diamond Foundations Needed for Paper Pieced Border Diamonds				
	5 Star Quilt	**6 Star Quilt**	**8 Star Quilt**	**12 Star Quilt**
Split Diamond Borders	16 L and 16 R	14 L and 14 R	20 L and 20 R	24 L and 24 R
Crazy Eights Borders	32 assorted	28 assorted	40 assorted	48 assorted

Customizing Your Quilt

Diamond Fabric Requirements for Diamond Borders, 6" Blocks				
(Measurements in yards unless otherwise indicated)				
	5 Star Quilt	6 Star Quilt	8 Star Quilt	12 Star Quilt
One-Color Diamonds	¼	¼	⅜	⅜
Two-Color Diamonds	⅛ each of 2	⅛ each of 2	¼ each of 2	¼ each of 2
Scrap or Crazy Eights Diamonds: assorted scraps totaling at least…	⅜	⅜	¾	⅞
Split Diamonds	¼ each of 2 (**A** and **C**)	¼ each of 2 (**A** and **C**)	⅜ each of 2 (**A** and **C**)	⅜ each of 2 (**A** and **C**)

Cutting Diamonds for One-Color Diamond Borders, 6" Blocks				
	5 Star Quilt	6 Star Quilt	8 Star Quilt	12 Star Quilt
Cut this many 1¾" strips across width:	3	3	3	4
Cut strips into this many 45° diamonds:	32	28	40	48

Cutting Diamonds for Two-Color Diamond Borders, 6" Blocks				
	5 Star Quilt	6 Star Quilt	8 Star Quilt	12 Star Quilt
Cut this many 1¾" strips across width from each fabric:	2	1	2	2
Cut strips into this many 45° diamonds of each fabric:	16	14	20	24

Cutting Diamonds for Scrap Diamond Borders, 6" Blocks				
	5 Star Quilt	6 Star Quilt	8 Star Quilt	12 Star Quilt
Cut this many 1¾", 45° diamonds from assorted fabrics:	32	28	40	48

Pre-Cutting Diamond Fabric for Split Diamond Borders, 6" Blocks				
	5 Star Quilt	6 Star Quilt	8 Star Quilt	12 Star Quilt
Cut this many 4¾" strips across width from each fabric (A and C):	1	2	2	2
Cut strips into this many 1¼" x 4¾" rectangles of each fabric:	32	28	40	48

Diamond Fabric Requirements for Diamond Borders, 12" Blocks

(Measurements in yards unless otherwise indicated)

	5 Star Quilt	6 Star Quilt	8 Star Quilt	12 Star Quilt
One-Color Diamonds	½	½	⅝	⅝
Two-Color Diamonds	⅜ each of 2	⅜ each of 2	⅜ each of 2	⅜ each of 2
Scrap or Crazy Eights Diamonds: assorted scraps totaling at least…	⅝	⅝	1⅜	1⅜
Split Diamonds	⅝ each of 2 (**A** and **C**)	⅝ each of 2 (**A** and **C**)	⅝ each of 2 (**A** and **C**)	¾ each of 2 (**A** and **C**)

Cutting Diamonds for One-Color Diamond Borders, 12" Blocks

	5 Star Quilt	6 Star Quilt	8 Star Quilt	12 Star Quilt
Cut this many 3" strips across width:	4	4	5	6
Cut strips into this many 45° diamonds:	32	28	40	48

Cutting Diamonds for Two-Color Diamond Borders, 12" Blocks

	5 Star Quilt	6 Star Quilt	8 Star Quilt	12 Star Quilt
Cut this many 3" strips across width from each fabric:	2	2	3	3
Cut strips into this many 45° diamonds of each fabric:	16	14	20	24

Cutting Diamonds for Scrap Diamond Borders, 12" Blocks

	5 Star Quilt	6 Star Quilt	8 Star Quilt	12 Star Quilt
Cut this many 3", 45° diamonds from assorted fabrics:	32	28	40	48

Pre-Cutting Diamond Fabric for Split Diamond Borders, 12" Blocks

	5 Star Quilt	6 Star Quilt	8 Star Quilt	12 Star Quilt
Cut this many 8" strips across width from each fabric (A and C):	2	2	2	3
Cut strips into this many 2" x 8" rectangles of each fabric:	32	28	40	48

General Instructions

Rotary Cutting Basic Shapes

Cutting Strips

Unless otherwise directed in the project instructions, begin with the fabric folded in half lengthwise, with selvages together. (The instructions are written for right-handed sewers. The illustrations show both right-handed and left-handed positions.)

Trim the right end of the fabric to get a smooth edge, perpendicular to the fold. Turn the fabric so the trimmed edge is to your left. Cut a strip across the width, using the strip-width measurement in your project directions. Cut additional strips as needed, taking care that the cuts remain perpendicular to the fold so the strips will be straight.

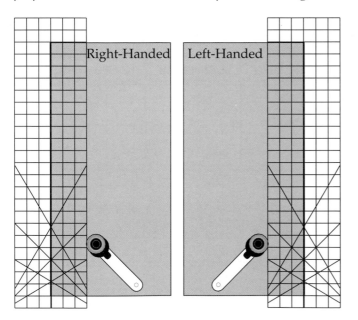

Unfold the strips. (The full width of the strip is not shown in the illustration.) You can stack several strips if desired. If the fabric has a directional print, take care to maintain the print orientation when placing the strips together.

Cutting Squares

Trim the layers at the right end of the strip set, cutting off any selvages. Carefully turn the strip set so the trimmed edge is to your left. Lay the ruler down and measure over from the trimmed edge, using the same measurement you used for the strip width, and cut to make a square.

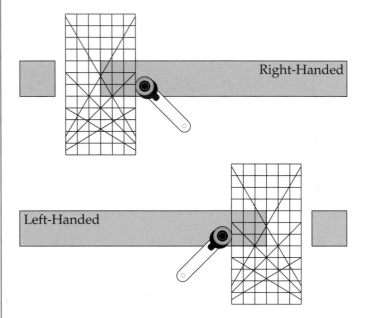

Cutting Half-Square Triangles

Cut a square once on the diagonal, aligning the 45° line along one edge for greater accuracy. This cut gives you two identical triangles. Each triangle will have the straight of grain on the two short sides and a bias edge on the long side.

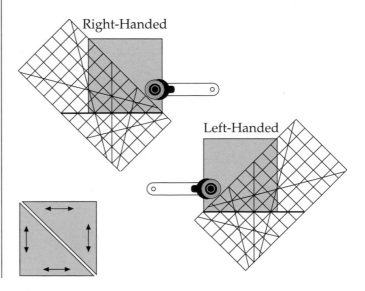

Stars a la Carte – Bethany S. Reynolds

Cutting Quarter-Square Triangles

Cut the square twice on the diagonal, aligning the 45° line along one edge for greater accuracy. These cuts give you four identical triangles. Each triangle will have the straight of grain on the long side and bias edges on the two short sides.

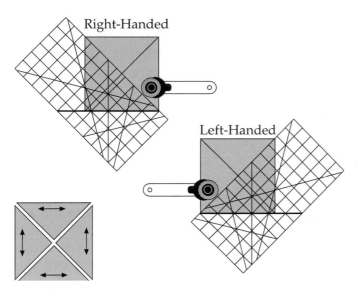

Cutting 45° Diamonds

Cut and stack strips as described previously. On the right end of the strip set, lay the ruler down with the 45° line along one long edge. Because the placement of the 45° line varies on different brands of rulers, your ruler may be positioned differently from the one in the illustration. Place the edge of the ruler far enough in to avoid the selvages. Cut along the edge through all layers. Set aside this first cut, which is scrap fabric.

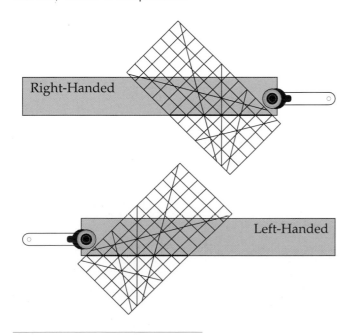

Carefully turn the strip set around so the angled edge is to your left. Lay the ruler down and measure over from the angled edge, using the same measurement you used for the strip width. Line up the vertical ruler line with the angled edge and the 45° line with one straight edge. Cut to make a diamond.

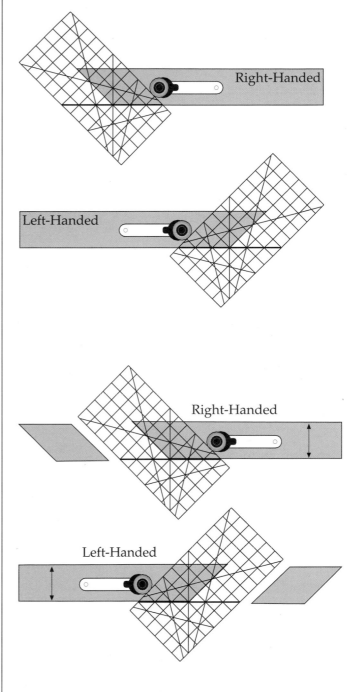

Paper Piecing Basics

The paper piecing instructions in the block chapters are necessarily brief. This section includes tips and techniques gathered from the author's experience, supplemented by many helpful suggestions from other quilters.

If you have never tried paper piecing, piece a sample diamond first, following the step-by-step directions given with each block design. You will find that the piecing goes quite quickly once you master the basics.

How Paper Piecing Works

• You will be piecing two fabrics with right sides together as in traditional piecing, but with an additional layer of paper on top to serve as a sewing guide and stabilizer. This paper will be removed later in the piecing process.

• In the method used in this book, the sewing is always done with the printed side of the paper on top and the fabric against the feed dogs.

• The finished diamond will be a mirror image of the foundation. Keep this in mind, especially when piecing identical blocks. If you forget which fabric you are using for each color area, turn a finished foundation or block wrong side up to see the positions of the fabrics during the piecing steps.

Preparing the Foundations

• Fabric foundations are not recommended for the projects in this book because they would create too much bulk at the centers of the stars.

• The foundation paper should be light enough to see the printed lines on the reverse side, and it should tear easily for removal after piecing. Lightweight copier paper is a readily available and inexpensive choice.

• Make photocopies or tracings of the foundations for your project. Photocopying is easier, faster, and usually more accurate. However, because some photocopy machines can distort the image, take care to check the copies for accuracy as follows:

Before making multiple copies for a project, make one copy and lay it over the original pattern. If there is any distortion, try a different copier. Even slight skewing of the foundations can cause problems later in the piecing process. Make all copies from the same master. Copies of photocopies are not as accurate.

• Cut the foundations apart. Leave a small margin of paper around the solid cutting line to ensure that you will have an accurate line for trimming after piecing. This margin is not shown in the illustrations.

Preparing the Fabrics

• Prewash your fabrics unless you are certain they are colorfast.

• For easier handling and greater control of off-grain edges, press the fabrics with spray sizing before cutting.

• Pre-cut fabrics for the patches for convenient piecing with less waste. The directions for each paper pieced diamond design in this book include pre-cutting instructions.

• If no pre-cutting instructions are given for your pattern or if you are using scraps, be generous in the size of the pre-cut patches. It is much easier to trim the pieces after sewing than to take out small stitches if a patch proves too small to cover the area.

Sewing Machine Setup

• Set your machine for straight stitching.

• Use a presser foot that offers good visibility.

• Set the stitch to a shorter than normal length (about 1.5 mm, or 14–16 stitches to the inch). Shorter stitches will make paper removal easier.

• For better stitch quality, use a sharp machine needle such as a quilting (H–Q) or jeans/denim (H–J) needle. I prefer a smaller needle size (70/10 or 80/12), especially when working on tightly woven fabrics like batiks.

• Use a good quality cotton or polyester thread in a neutral color that will blend with your fabric.

Using the Foundation Numbers

• The foundations are numbered for piecing order. The numbers refer to the patch areas, not to the seam lines. You will always begin by piecing the seam between area #1 and area #2.

• In this book, the numbers on the foundations are rotated so that the number for the area you are covering will appear upright when the foundation is under the presser foot. You can tell which way to turn the foundation for the next seam by turning it until the next number is upright. The seam line will be to the left of the number. The area the patch will cover will be to the right of the presser foot.

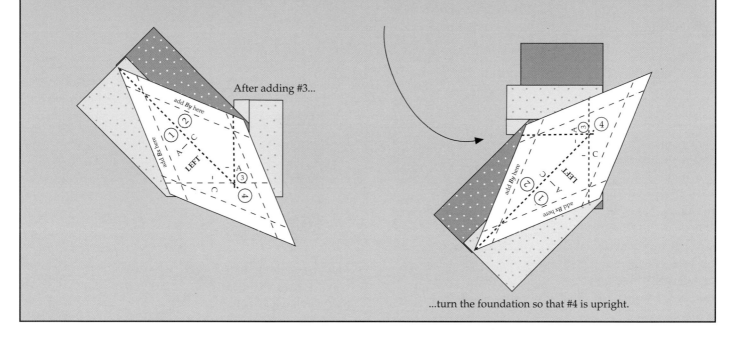

After adding #3...

...turn the foundation so that #4 is upright.

Pressing Issues

• After folding each new patch in place, flatten the seam carefully. Make sure there are no creases or pleats because these may prevent points from meeting correctly in the finished block.

• Avoid using an iron on paper foundations because it may smudge the foundation lines or distort the paper. A fingernail usually works well for pressing seams during construction, or you can use a "wooden iron" (see Sources, page 127, or make your own by using one half of a wooden spring-type clothespin). However, some fabrics may not cooperate with just finger pressing. If you find it necessary to use an iron, use a low setting without steam. Press only on the fabric side and cover your ironing surface to protect it from ink transfer.

• Take care to press only on the seam line. Avoid stretching the unsewn edges of the patch.

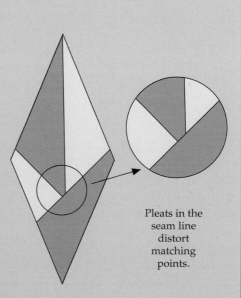

Pleats in the seam line distort matching points.

General Instructions

The Butterfly Trick

Try this technique to make sure the fabric you are adding will cover the color area when it is pressed over it.

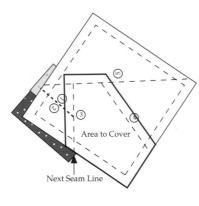

Look for the next area to be covered, including a seam allowance. In this illustration, it is area #3, shown by the bold outline.

Think of this shape as one wing of a butterfly, with the seam line as the body. Visualize the shape of the second wing of the butterfly, a mirror image of the first. It is this shape that the next fabric patch must cover.

Imagine now that the butterfly's wings are closing. Fold the foundation over on the next seam line, extending the fold to the edge of the foundation. Trim the excess fabric to ¼" to create a straight edge for lining up the next piece of fabric.

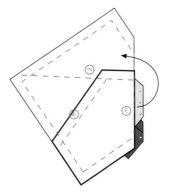

Lay the next piece of fabric under the foundation, with the right side of the fabric facing up and a straight edge aligned with the trimmed edges. The wing of the butterfly must fit on the fabric.

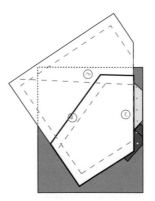

Unfold the foundation and stitch along the seam line.

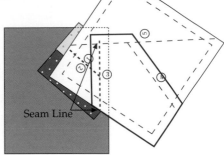

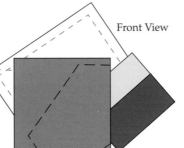

Press the new piece of fabric over the area. The butterfly's wings are closed again.

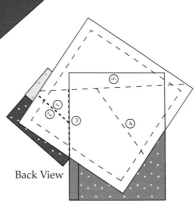

This trick will help you use your scraps to best advantage, especially when you are working with odd shapes and angles.

Examples of different shapes.

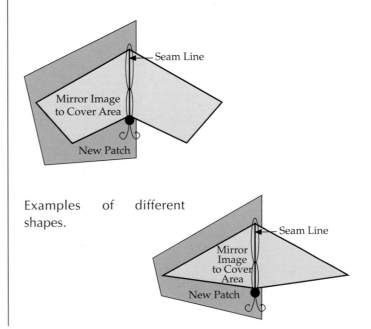

Pieced Triangle Squares

There are a number of ways to piece squares from two right triangles of fabric. The samples in this book were made using the grid method, and the yardages have been calculated based on this method. You can, of course, use another technique if you have one you prefer. The yardages should be sufficient to cover most techniques, but to be safe, allow a little extra fabric if you plan to use another method.

Making Pieced Squares with the Grid Method

The grid method is a simple way to make multiple pieced squares from two fabrics. Each square in the grid will yield two pieced squares. While the grid can be any size, a grid that is an odd number of squares in at least one direction, such as a 3 x 4 grid, is convenient because it can be sewn with a continuous stitching line.

Marking the Grid

To prepare the grid, first determine the finished size of the pieced squares, excluding the seam allowance. For example, the illustrations here show the square units needed for the 6" Night and Noon Pinwheel block. In the finished block, each pieced square unit will need to measure 3". Add 1" to this measurement to determine the grid size, which is 4" in this example.

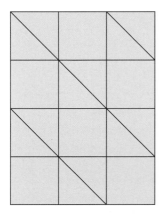

On the reverse side of one fabric, draw a 3 x 4 square grid in the required size. Use a pencil, washable marker, or permanent pen. Beginning in one corner, draw a diagonal line through the grid squares. Draw two more diagonal lines in the same direction as shown. At this point, every other square should have a line through it, and the alternate squares should be unmarked.

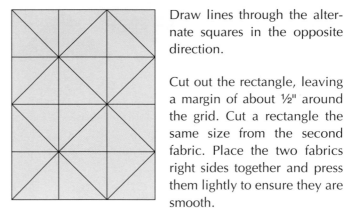

Draw lines through the alternate squares in the opposite direction.

Cut out the rectangle, leaving a margin of about ½" around the grid. Cut a rectangle the same size from the second fabric. Place the two fabrics right sides together and press them lightly to ensure they are smooth.

Sewing

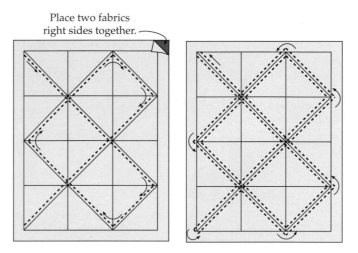

Place two fabrics right sides together.

Begin sewing in one corner. Stitch ¼" to the left of the diagonal line and pivot at each corner, as shown by the arrows. When you reach the end of the continuous line, pivot around the end and continue back down the other side of the diagonal line, back to the beginning point.

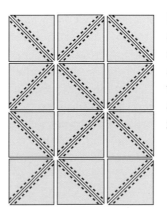

Press the pieced rectangle again if it has puckered during sewing. Trim off the margin around the rectangle and cut the triangles apart, cutting on all the diagonal and straight grid lines.

General Instructions

You can press the seam allowances open or to one side. To press the units open while pressing the allowance toward the dark side, 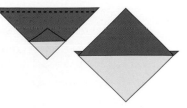 lay them down with the darker fabric on top. Use the tip of the iron to flip up the dark triangle. Press lightly along the seam line, taking care not the distort the square.

Trimming the Pieced Squares

These squares will be slightly larger than needed and should be trimmed to the correct size before they are pieced together. The trimming step also removes the "dog ears" in the corners. Note that the trimmed square must include a seam allowance. In the example here, the units need to measure 3½" to produce the desired 3" finished size.

Measurement lines for trimmed size of square should fall within the square.

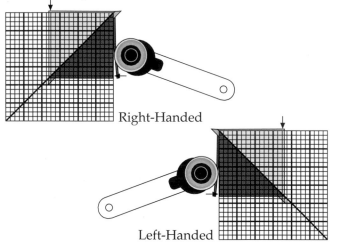

Right-Handed

Left-Handed

To trim a pieced square, use a square rotary cutting ruler with a diagonal (bias) line. If the ruler's numbers begin in one corner, place that corner on the upper-right corner of the square if you are right-handed. If you are left-handed, the numbers on the ruler should start at the upper-left corner. Place the diagonal line of the ruler on the seam line of the pieced square. Place the measurement lines for the trimmed size, including seam allowances, so that they fall within the pieced square unit. The pieced square should extend beyond the ruler a bit on each side of the corner. Trim these two edges.

Place measurement lines for trimmed size of square on the trimmed edges.

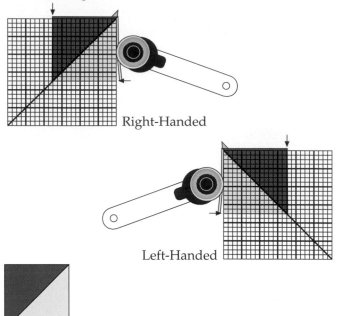

Right-Handed

Left-Handed

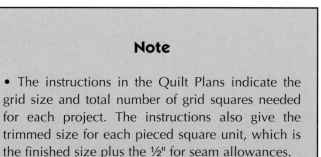

Turn the pieced unit 180° so that the two trimmed edges will be under the ruler. Lay the ruler down again with the diagonal line on the seam line. Line up the measurements for the trimmed size on the two trimmed edges of the pieced unit. Trim the two remaining edges. The pieced square unit should then be the desired size.

Note

• The instructions in the Quilt Plans indicate the grid size and total number of grid squares needed for each project. The instructions also give the trimmed size for each pieced square unit, which is the finished size plus the ½" for seam allowances.

• Use a ¼" presser foot or experiment to find the ¼" distance on your standard presser foot, because the needle plate will be hidden. A scant ¼" is preferable to a generous one for this method.

General Instructions for Appliqué

In the Quilt Plans, the background blocks are cut slightly larger than needed because the appliqué may draw the fabric in a bit. The blocks should be trimmed after completing the appliqué and any embroidery.

The appliqué designs are given on pages 120–125. Follow the instructions for copying and enlarging the designs, as necessary.

Preparing the Appliqué Pieces

For best results, prewash and press all background and appliqué fabrics.

Two methods of preparing and positioning the pieces for machine appliqué are given. You can use any method you like. If you prefer to appliqué by hand, remember to add a turn-under allowance to each piece as you cut it.

Paper-Backed Fusing Web Method

This method is quick and simple. It stabilizes the fabrics well for machine appliqué and helps to keep the raw fabric edges secure. You can use any brand of paper-backed fusing web. The yardage charts in the Quilt Plan chapter list the approximate yardages required for this method. These yardages are based on an 11"-wide web. You may need less if you are using a wider one.

For the laurel appliqué designs, make a plastic or cardboard stencil of the leaf shape. Using the stencil, trace the leaves as close together as possible to conserve fabric and fusing web. You do not need to mark the embroidery lines.

For the Leaf Wreath block, trace the wreaths on the paper side of the fusing web. You can trace directly from the design. The finished appliqué will be a mirror image, which will make the leaves rotate counterclockwise as shown in the Waste Not, Want More quilt. Make one tracing for each block. You do not need to trace the embroidery lines. Cut the wreath tracings apart, leaving a margin of paper around each wreath design. Do not cut right on the lines, yet.

Fuse the paper-backed web to the wrong side of the appliqué fabric. Follow the manufacturer's instructions carefully because brands vary greatly in application requirements. Cut out the appliqué pieces on the traced lines.

Freezer-Paper and Basting-Spray or Glue-Stick Method

This method is a bit more involved, and because the raw edges are not permanently fused in place, it is not as durable as the method described previously. However, it eliminates the need for fusing web and produces appliqué that is soft and flexible like hand appliqué.

You will need plastic-coated freezer paper for this technique. The plastic coating softens when the paper is pressed at a low setting with a dry iron, allowing the paper to adhere temporarily to fabric. You should be able to peel the paper off the fabric easily. Before beginning your project, test the freezer paper on a scrap of fabric to determine the correct temperature and length of time needed to achieve a temporary bond.

For the laurel appliqué designs, trace a number of leaf shapes on the dull side of the freezer paper. You do not need to trace the embroidery lines. The freezer paper pieces can be reused several times.

For the Leaf Wreath block, you will need to reverse the design if you want to have the leaves rotate counterclockwise as in the sample quilt. Trace the design on lightweight paper and redraw the lines on the reverse side or have the design reversed at a copy shop.

Lay the freezer paper over the traced design with the dull side up. Make one tracing for each block. You do not need to trace the embroidery lines. Cut the wreath tracings apart, leaving a margin of paper around each wreath design. Do not cut on the lines, yet.

Place the shiny side of the freezer-paper tracing against the right side of the appliqué fabric. Press on the paper side with a dry iron at a low setting. The paper should adhere easily. If it does not, set the temperature slightly higher and check again with scraps.

Cut out the appliqué pieces on the traced lines. If you leave the freezer paper on the appliqué pieces until they are in place on the block, they will be easier to handle.

Positioning the Appliqué

To mark the position for the appliqué design on the block,

General Instructions

fold each background fabric square in quarters and lightly press the folds. Unfold the block and fold again on each diagonal, pressing lightly to mark each one. Mark the center point of each block with chalk or a washable marker as well because you will need to refer to it for trimming later.

Fusing Web Method: Peel off the paper backing before positioning the pieces.

Freezer Paper Method: Spray the back of each appliqué piece with fabric basting spray (see Sources, page 127) or use a small amount of glue stick on the back of each piece before positioning them.

If you are using a light background fabric, you may be able to place the appliqué pieces by laying the appliqué design underneath the background fabric square wrong side up. If you cannot see through the background fabric, you can use a light box or try the following method:

Trace the block design on a lightweight non-woven material, such as non-fusible interfacing or tear-away sewing stabilizer. The material should be thin enough to see the appliqué fabrics when they are placed underneath and should be able to withstand medium heat. Mark the center and placement lines and embroidery on the tracing.

Place the tracing over the background fabric block, centering the design. Pin at two adjacent corners. Lift the tracing and slide the appliqué pieces underneath. Adjust them until they are in position.

Fusing Web Method: Press lightly at a low setting to tack the pieces in place. Remove the tracing and press securely, following the fusing web manufacturer's directions.

Freezer Paper Method: Finger press the pieces in place. Remove the tracing and carefully peel off the freezer paper from each piece. If any pieces move during this step, lay the tracing down again and adjust as necessary. Press, using a press cloth, to smooth the pieces without disturbing the placement.

Stitching the Appliqué

Machine appliqué the blocks with a zigzag satin stitch, blind hem, or blanket stitch. Use matching or invisible thread for a hand appliquéd effect or use a decorative thread, if you prefer. If you aren't familiar with your sewing machine's appliqué settings, check the owner's manual or consult your machine dealer for recommended

stitches and setup. Do a test on scraps to find the settings you like best for stitch width, stitch length, and thread tension. If the stitch puckers, try using a tear-away stabilizer under the block.

Appliqué a sample leaf or two to check your thread choices and stitch settings. Decide on a technique for turning neatly at the tips. Here are some options:

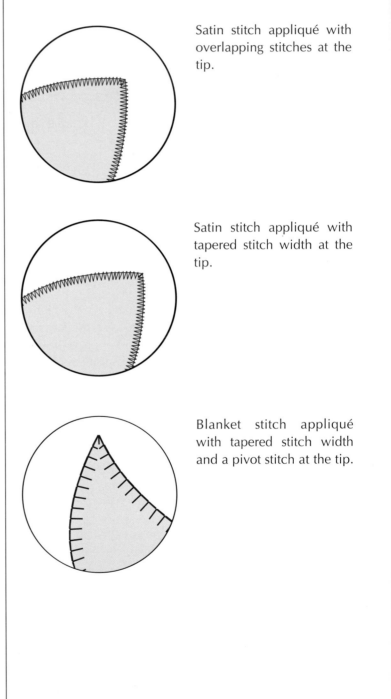

Satin stitch appliqué with overlapping stitches at the tip.

Satin stitch appliqué with tapered stitch width at the tip.

Blanket stitch appliqué with tapered stitch width and a pivot stitch at the tip.

Adding Embroidery or Quilting

Laurel Appliqué Designs

The straight stems and veins on the leaves can be embroidered by hand or machine. In STRIPE IT RICH (page 80), the stem is a length of heavy decorative rayon thread couched in place with a zigzag stitch. The triple straight stitch or stretch straight stitch available on many sewing machines is another good option.

Mark the stems and veins with a straight-edge and chalk or another removable marking device. Experiment with thread and stitch choices on scrap fabric before embroidering the blocks.

Leaf Wreath Design

The veins on each leaf can be embroidered by hand or machine before the quilt is layered, or they can be formed by quilted stitches after layering. In WASTE NOT, WANT MORE (page 35), the veins were hand quilted with a heavy cotton thread by using large stitches for a folk-art look.

If you choose to embroider the veins, mark them on the leaves freehand or use the placement guide. Use chalk or another removable marking device. Experiment with thread and stitch choices on scrap fabric, and then embroider.

Trimming the Appliqué Blocks

Press the completed appliqué blocks on a padded surface, such as a towel. Use a press cloth if you have delicate embroidery or other embellishments.

Square blocks should be trimmed to 6½" for the 6" block quilt plans, or 12½" for the 12" block plans. If the blocks require trimming, it's best to use a square ruler. Place the 3¼" mark (6" finished blocks) or 6¼" mark (12" finished blocks) on the center point of the square and trim two sides. Turn the square a half-turn and trim the other two sides. This method ensures that the appliqué design will still be centered after trimming.

For the side and corner blocks in the On-Point Quilt Plans, follow the trimming instructions with the appliqué designs on pages 120–125.

Quilting Design Ideas

A carefully chosen, well-executed quilting design often makes the difference between a good quilt and an outstanding one. Quilting creates dimension and texture through the play of light and shadow on the surface. You can use quilting to your advantage, drawing a viewer's eye to the aspects of the quilt you want to highlight, while de-emphasizing areas that are less important.

A detailed description of quilting methods would fill another book, and there are many good references available on this topic (see Bibliography, page 127). Rather than giving you general quilting information, I'd like to provide you with some specific advice about quilting the projects in this book.

As you quilt your project, remember one key point of quilting design: The areas that come forward and attract the viewer are the areas that you do not quilt. Quilting flattens the surface and makes the unquilted areas raise up. If you have an area you'd like to feature, quilt around it.

Quilting the Stars

To keep the stars shining brightly as the focal point of your quilt, begin by outline quilting the star points. Quilting ⅛" – ¼" away from the seams in the background fabric will help to make the stars stand out from the background. Quilting in the seam line is another option, but it is less effective for creating visual depth. It will, however, help to define the star points, and it may be the best solution for quilt plans such as Stargazer, in which quilting outside the seam line would extend into the setting pieces.

The 6" star blocks may not need any additional quilting, although you may want to tack down the centers of the stars with a few machine or hand stitches. YANKEE THRIFT (page 68) has red embroidery floss tacks at the center of each star and in the corners of the block.

Quilting within the star will enhance the star blocks and will keep the 12" blocks looking crisp. Full-size quilting designs are given on page 119. Designs A and B help to break up basic unpieced Diamond Stars, creating the illusion of more complicated piecing. Design B also works well for the borders on the Diamond Border Quilt Plans.

For the pieced diamond stars, outlining some or all of the interior seams will emphasize the piecing design.

Quilting the Setting and Background Areas

If you have used a setting with pieced alternate blocks or pieced borders, consider some outline quilting to delineate these design areas.

Quilting down the background areas will help to highlight the blocks, making them "pop" from the surface. Quilting also helps to hide the seams in the background areas and integrates the stars with their setting.

Allover quilting, such as machine stippling or other filler patterns, can be used to cover background areas. NURSERY STARS (page 39) shows how a simple background quilting design can create surface interest.

If you have plain alternate blocks in your quilt, you may want to use a quilting motif in these. The Leaf Wreath and Laurel Appliqué designs (pages 120–125) can be used as quilting designs. CELESTIAL NAVIGATION (page 76) shows the Leaf Wreath quilting design.

Bindings, Sleeves, and Labels

Bindings

Bindings add strength to the edges of a quilt. A bias-cut binding is essential for quilts with curved edges, such as STRIPE IT RICH (page 80). For quilts with straight edges, however, a straight-grain binding can be used, and this type is easier to handle than bias binding. You can use the same fabric as your outer border or provide a little accent with a contrasting binding.

Cut your straight-grain binding strips on the lengthwise or crosswise grain of the fabric. For a ⅜" finished binding, cut 2½" strips. Piece together enough strips to make a binding long enough to go around the perimeter of the quilt, including about 12" for turning corners and finishing the ends.

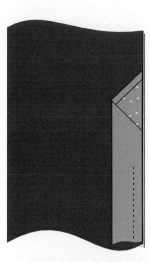

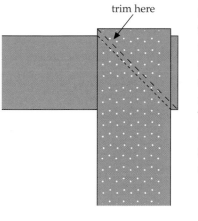

trim here

Piecing the strips together with a diagonal seam line will stagger the seam allowances for a smoother binding. Trim the excess fabric, leaving ¼" allowances and press the seam allowances open.

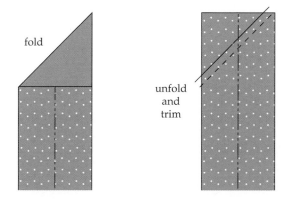

fold

unfold and trim

After piecing all the strips together to make one long strip, press the binding strip in half lengthwise, wrong sides together. Press one end at a right angle and trim the extra fabric to ¼" from the fold line.

If you want to add a sleeve for hanging your quilt, read the section about sleeves, starting on page 104, before sewing on the binding.

To attach the binding, beginning part way down one side of your quilt, place the folded binding strip on the quilt top, right sides together with raw edges aligned. Leave about 3" unsewn at the beginning of the binding to allow for finishing. Sew the binding in place with a ⅜" seam allowance (on most machines, the width of the all-purpose presser foot will be about right).

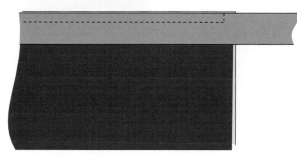

As you approach each corner, stop stitching ⅜" from the raw edge of the quilt top at the corner. With the needle down, turn the quilt a quarter turn. Backstitch straight back to the raw edge of the quilt and raise the needle and the presser foot.

Fold the binding up at a 45° angle and then down, matching the second fold to the raw edge of the quilt. Begin stitching at the folded edge of the binding and continue to the next corner.

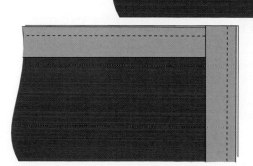

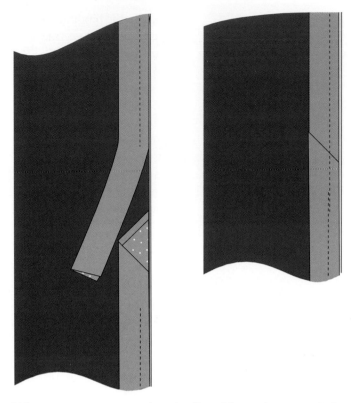

When you come around to the first side again, stop stitching 3" or 4" from the beginning end. Lay the tail end along the raw edge, overlapping the beginning angled end and smooth the ends in place. Cut the tail end so that it overlaps the beginning end by ¼" to ½". Tuck the tail end into the beginning end. Finish stitching the binding in place.

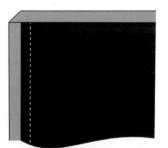

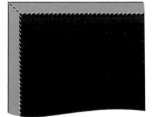

Bring the folded edge of the binding around to the back and blind stitch it in place, tucking in the corners to form neat miters. Blind stitch the angled edge where the ends meet.

Sleeves

If you plan to hang your quilt or enter it in a show, consider adding a hanging sleeve as you sew the binding. This method saves time and results in a sleeve that will evenly distribute the weight of the quilt.

Prepare the sleeve by cutting a rectangle of fabric that is about 2" shorter than the width of the quilt. The sleeve width should be about 12" for bed quilts. For small wall quilts, 8" will suffice. Hem the short ends of the sleeve and press it in half lengthwise, wrong sides together.

Add the binding to the front of the quilt, but don't bring the folded edge around to the back, yet. On the back of the quilt, center the sleeve along the top edge and pin it in place. Stitch it to the quilt with a scant ⅜" seam, just inside the binding seam line. Bring the binding around to the back and finish as directed previously, catching the sleeve and the quilt back as you finish the top edge.

Blind stitch the bottom layer of the ends of the sleeve and the folded edge of the sleeve to the quilt back.

Labels

Label your quilt with your name, the date, and any other information you feel is important. If the quilt is to be a gift, you may want to add information on how to care for the quilt. As a security measure if the quilt will be exhibited, consider labeling the quilt in permanent ink underneath a sewn fabric label.

Labels can be as simple or as elaborate as you like. Your descendants and future quilters will be grateful that you provided this information.

Foundations

6" Whirligig Star Foundations

Use 4 left and 4 right diamonds per block.

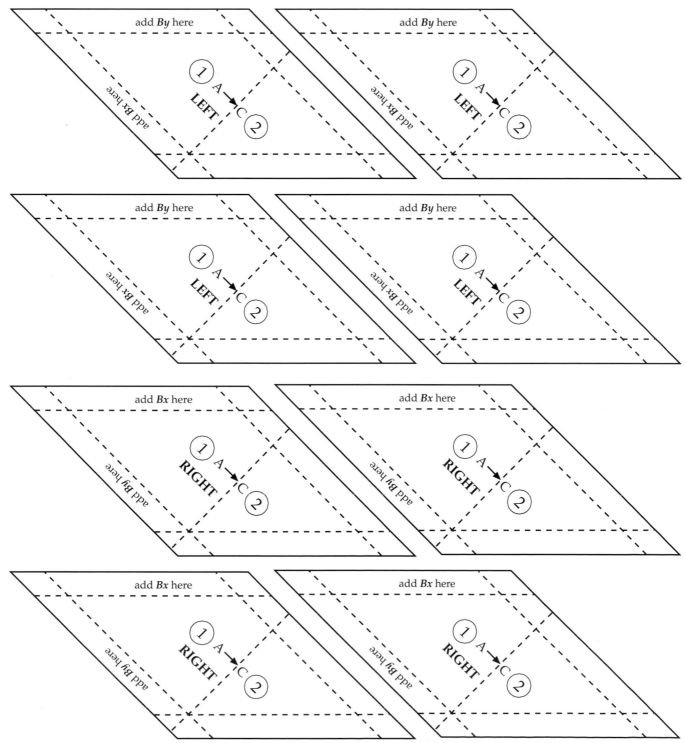

12" Whirligig Star Foundations

Use 4 left and 4 right diamonds per block.

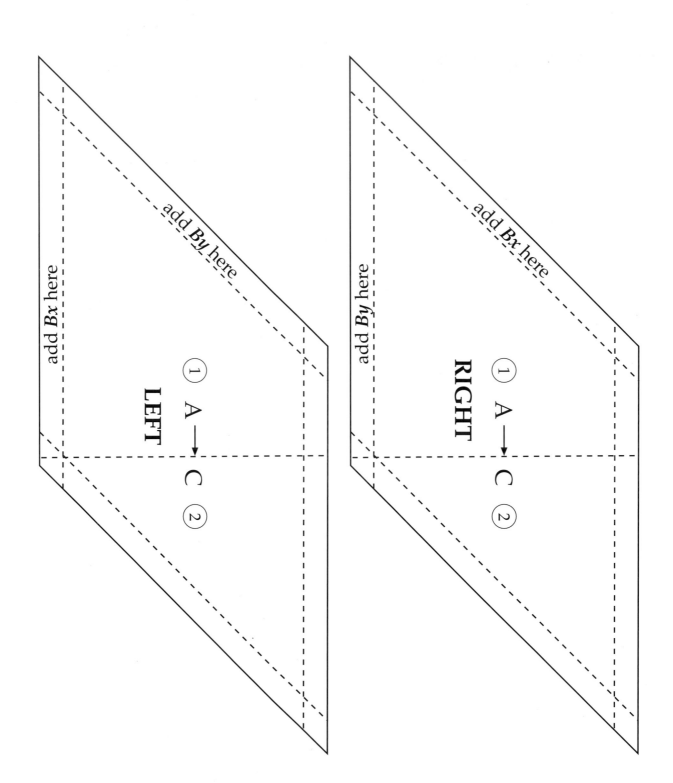

6" Split Star Foundations

Use 4 left and 4 right diamonds per block.

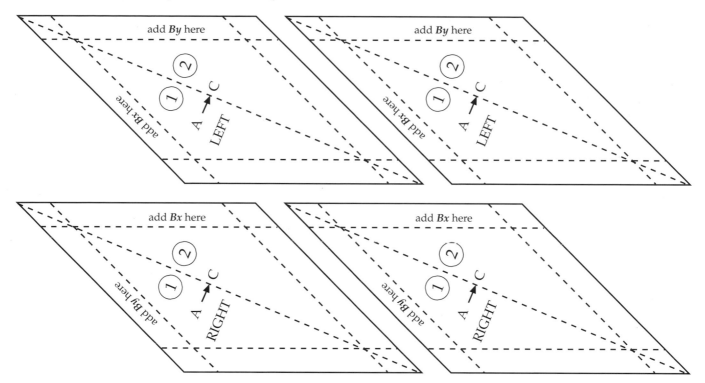

6" Compass Star Foundations

Use 4 left and 4 right diamonds per block.

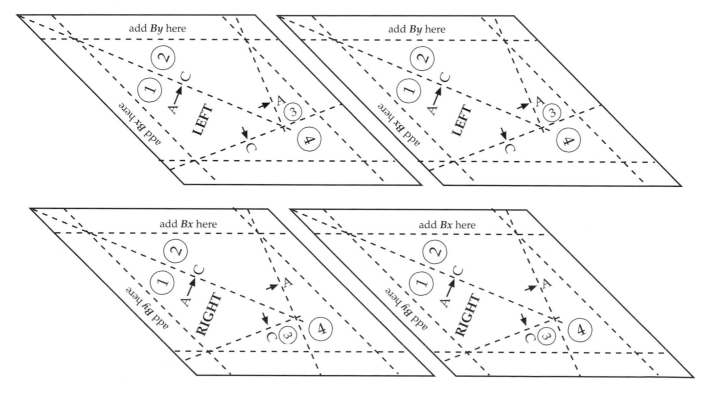

12" Split Star Foundations

Use 4 left and 4 right diamonds per block.

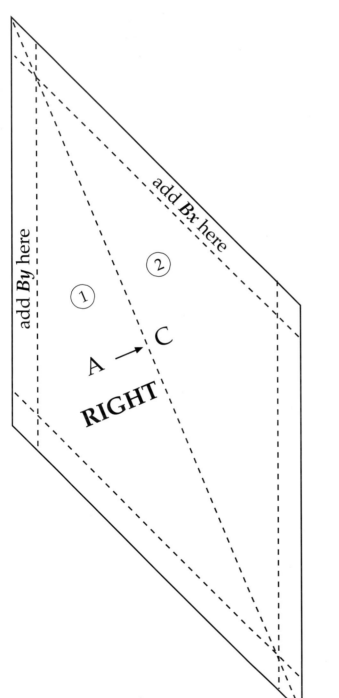

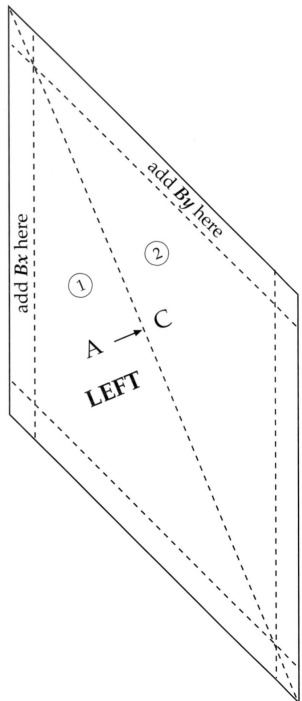

12" Compass Star Foundations
Use 4 left and 4 right diamonds per block.

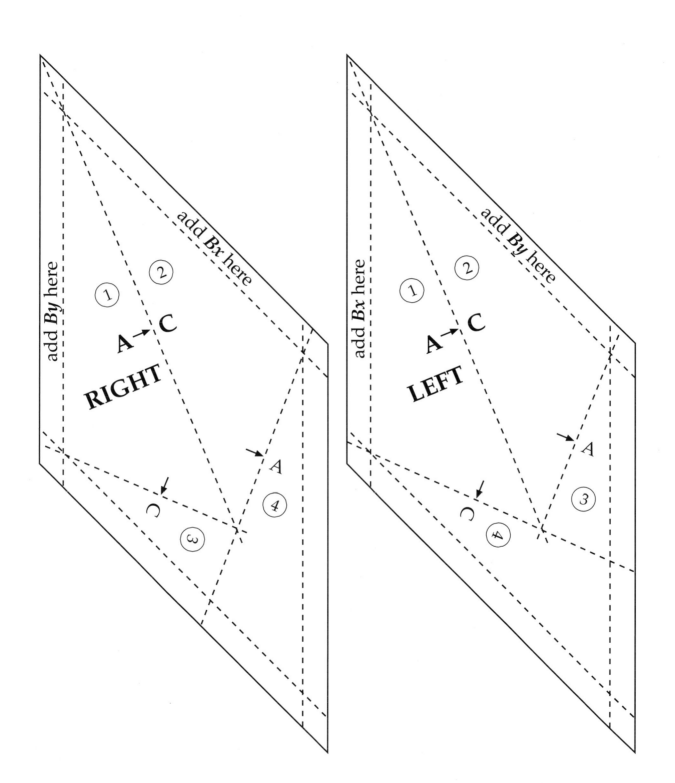

6" Crazy Eights Foundations
Use 8 assorted diamonds per block.

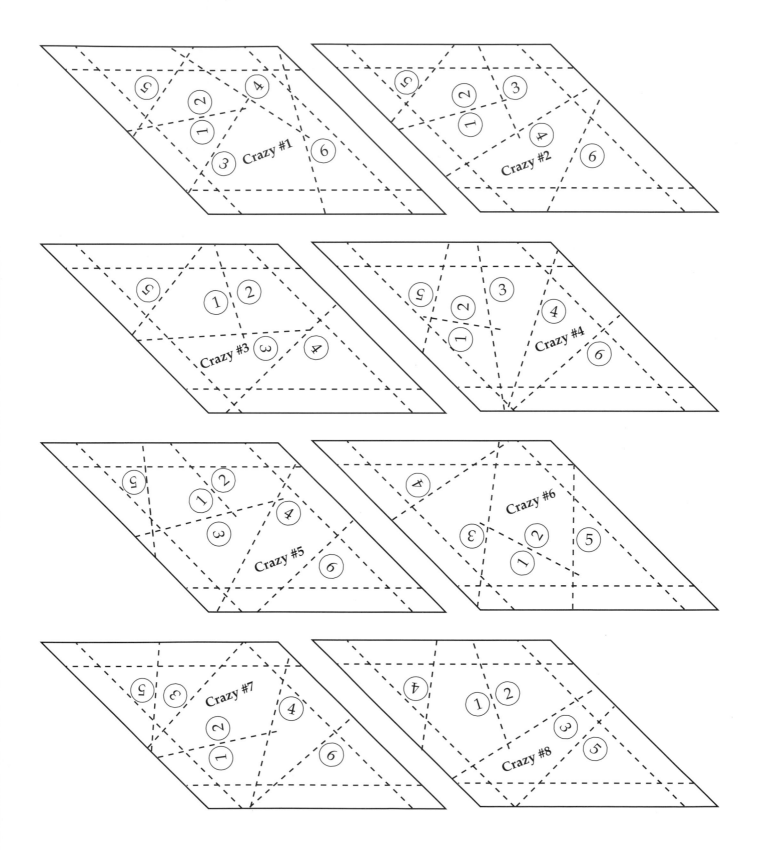

Stars a la Carte – Bethany S. Reynolds

12" Crazy Eights Foundations
Use 8 assorted diamonds per block.

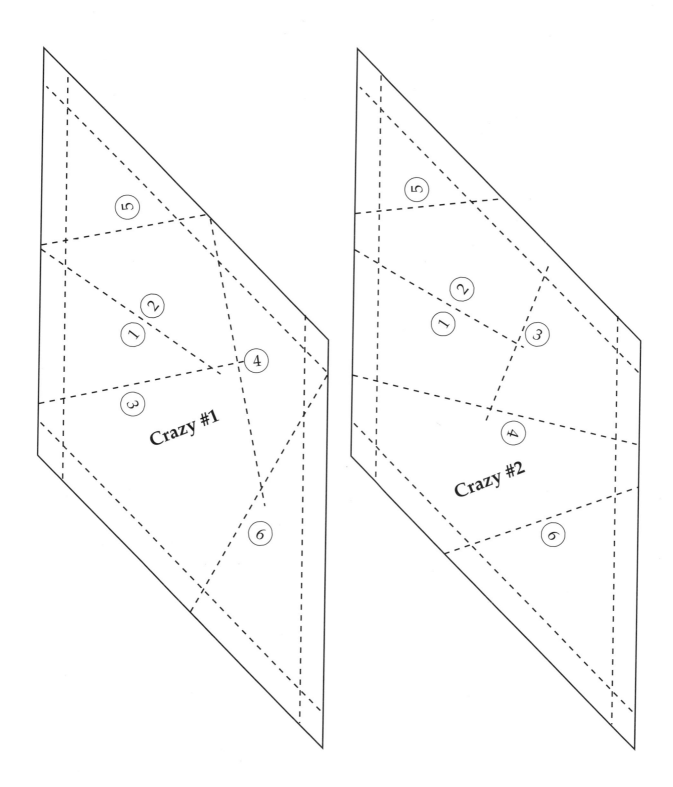

12" Crazy Eights Foundations
Use 8 assorted diamonds per block.

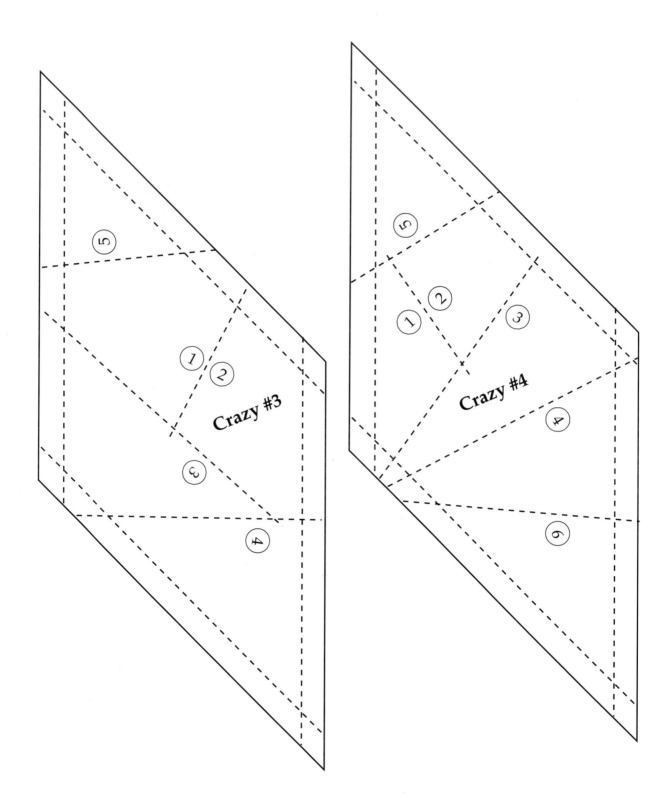

Crazy #3

Crazy #4

Stars a la Carte – Bethany S. Reynolds

12" Crazy Eights Foundations
Use 8 assorted diamonds per block.

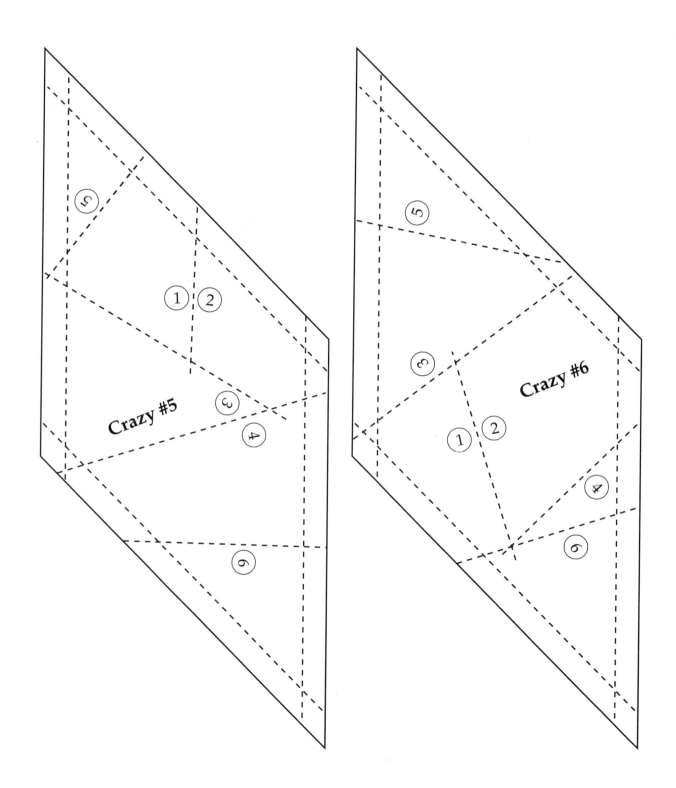

12" Crazy Eights Foundations

Use 8 assorted diamonds per block.

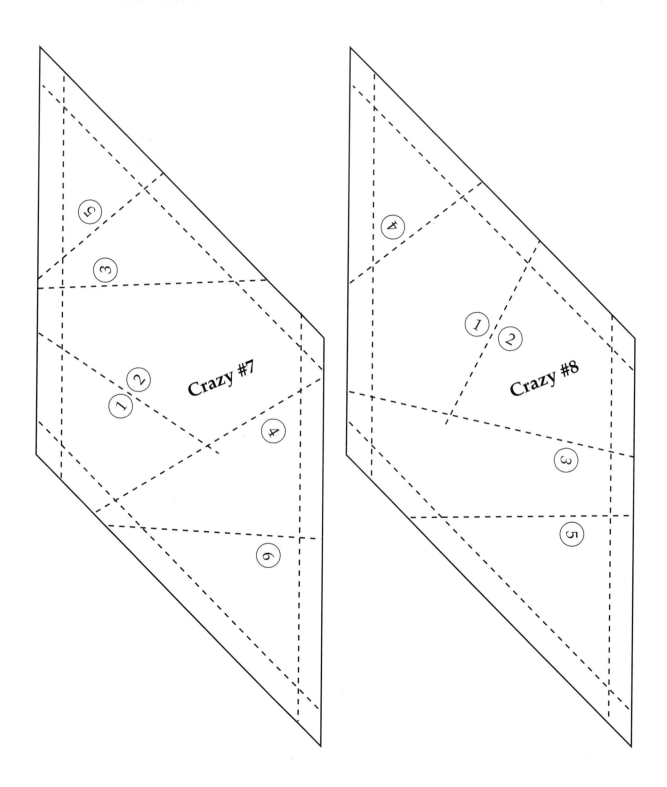

Crazy #7

Crazy #8

12" Swallowtail Foundations
Use 4 units per block.

6" Swallowtail Foundations
Use 4 units per block.
(page 116)

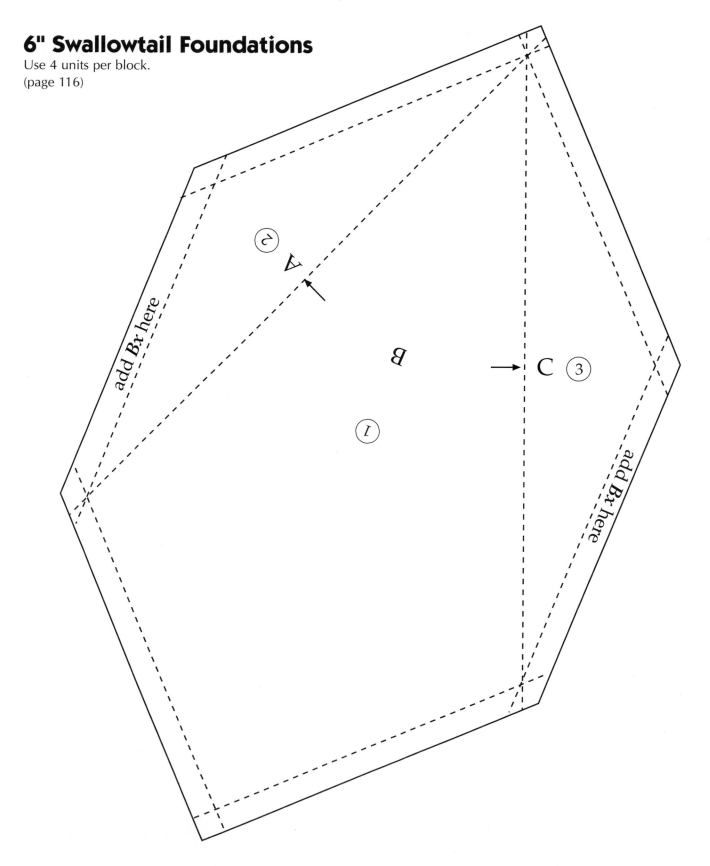

Foundations

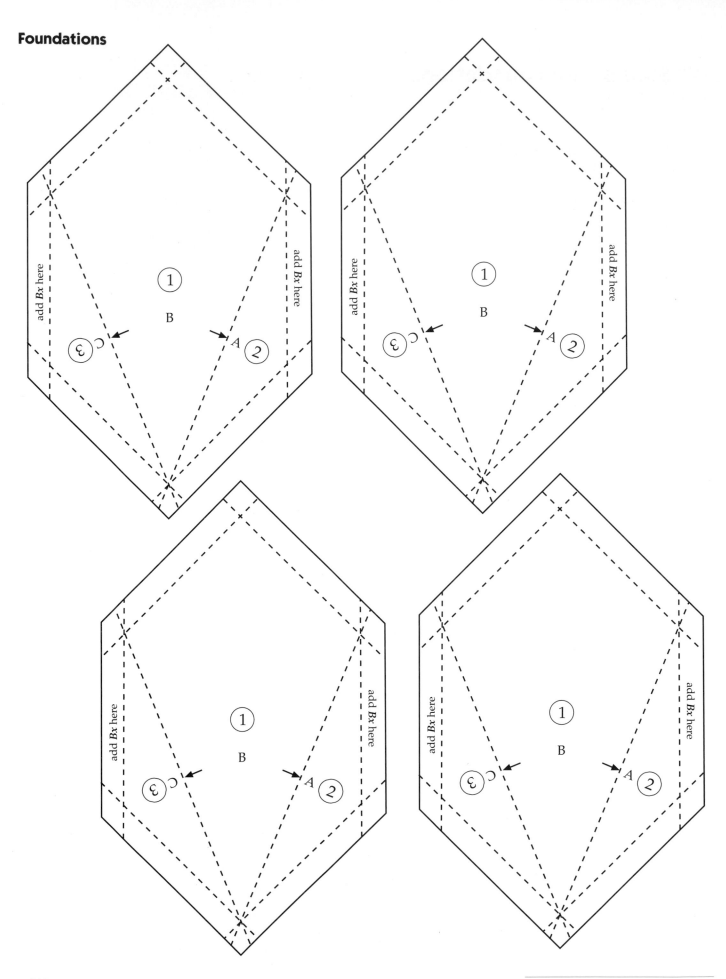

Stars a la Carte – Bethany S. Reynolds

6" Split Diamond Border Block Foundations

Use 1 left and 1 right diamond per block. Use these foundations only for the border blocks. Foundations for the 6" Split Star are on page 107.

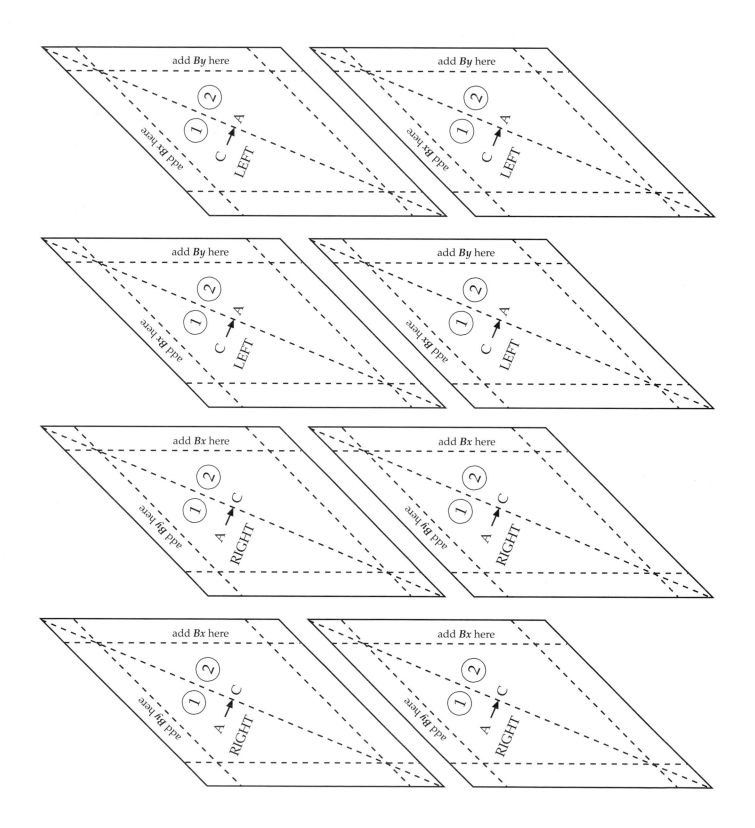

12" Split Diamond Border Block Foundations

Use 1 left and 1 right diamond per block. Use these foundations only for the border blocks. Foundations for the 12" Split Star are on page 108.

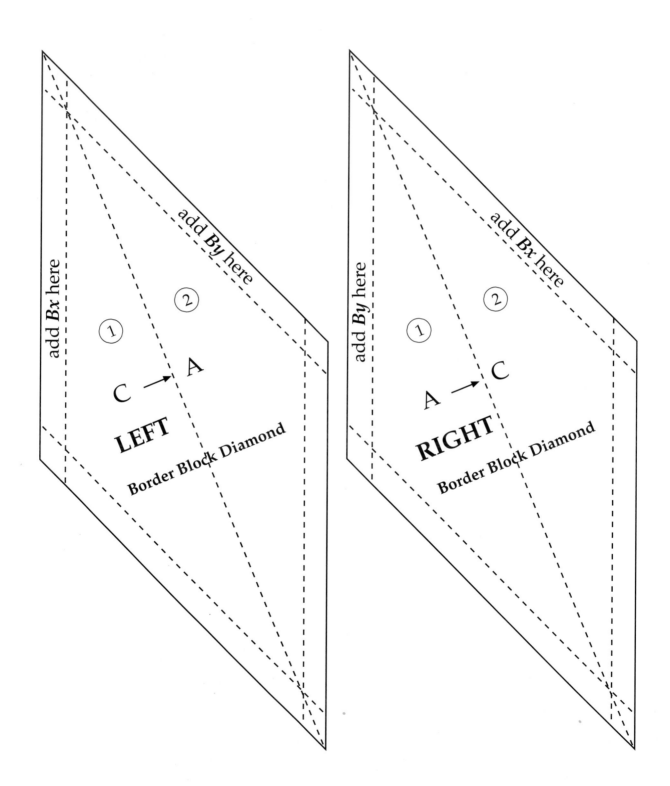

Part Six Quilting and Appliqué Designs Part Six

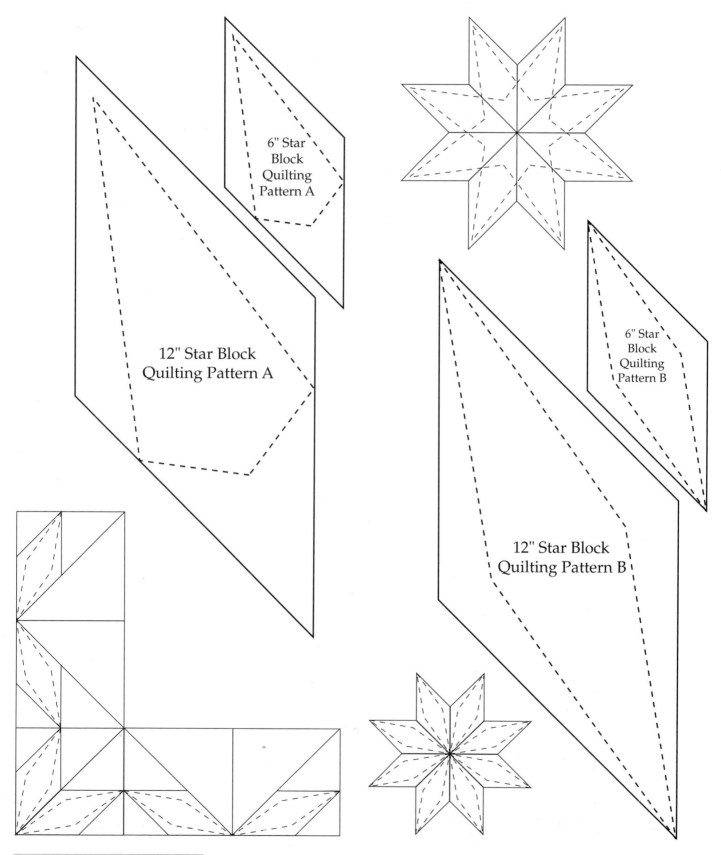

6" Star Block Quilting Pattern A

12" Star Block Quilting Pattern A

6" Star Block Quilting Pattern B

12" Star Block Quilting Pattern B

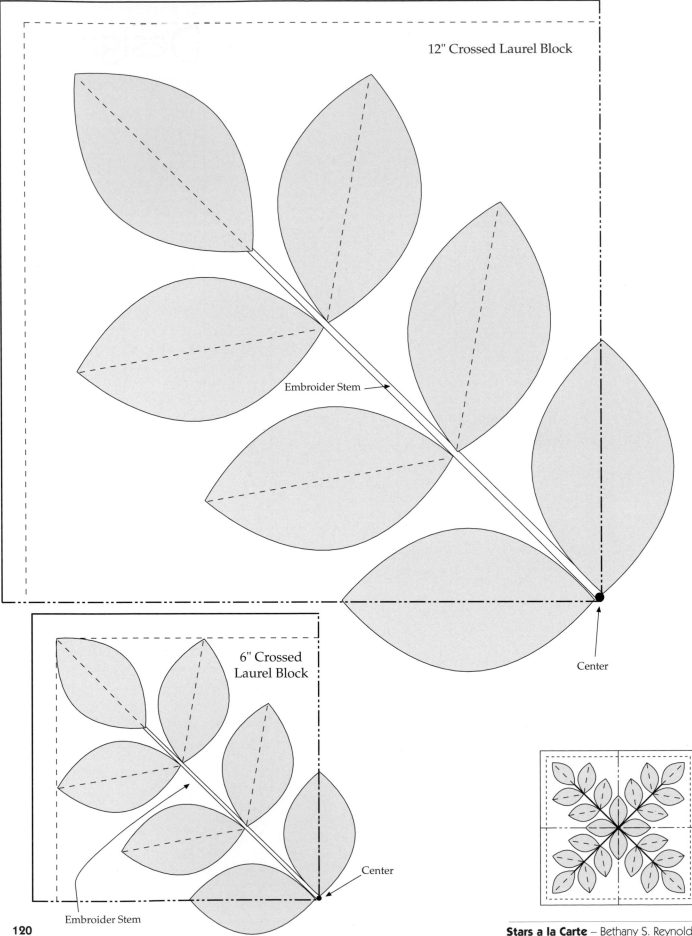

12" Crossed Laurel Block

Embroider Stem

Center

6" Crossed
Laurel Block

Center

Embroider Stem

Stars a la Carte – Bethany S. Reynolds

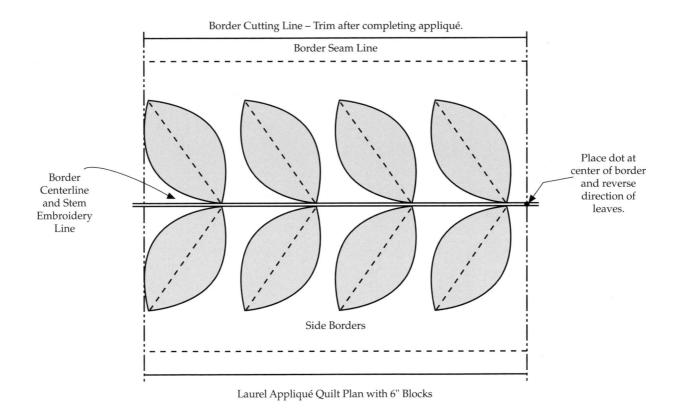

Border Cutting Line – Trim after completing appliqué.

Border Seam Line

Border Centerline and Stem Embroidery Line

Place dot at center of border and reverse direction of leaves.

Side Borders

Laurel Appliqué Quilt Plan with 6" Blocks

Quilt Plan with 6" Blocks

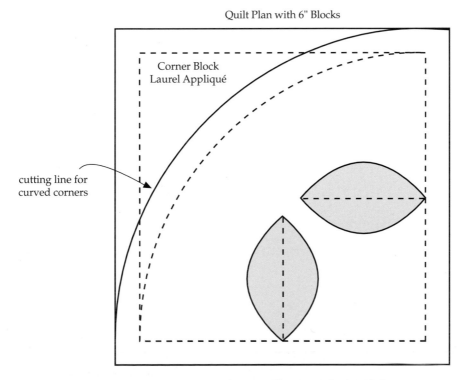

Corner Block Laurel Appliqué

cutting line for curved corners

Corners can be rounded or square.

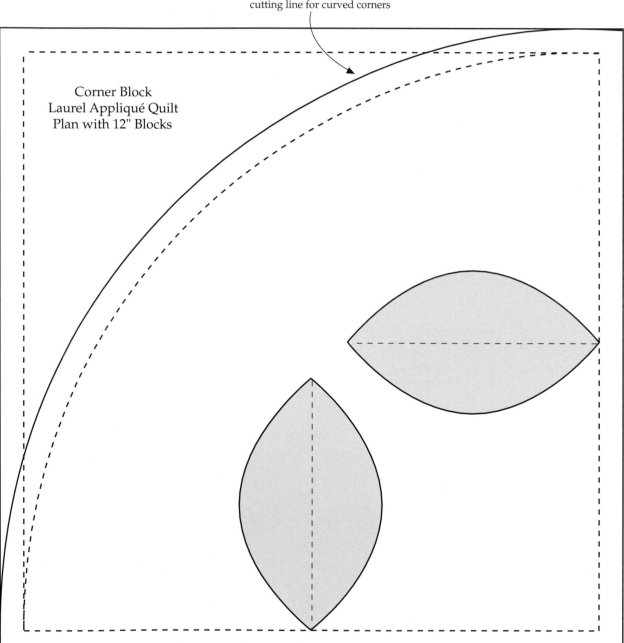

cutting line for curved corners

Corner Block
Laurel Appliqué Quilt
Plan with 12" Blocks

Corners can be rounded or square.

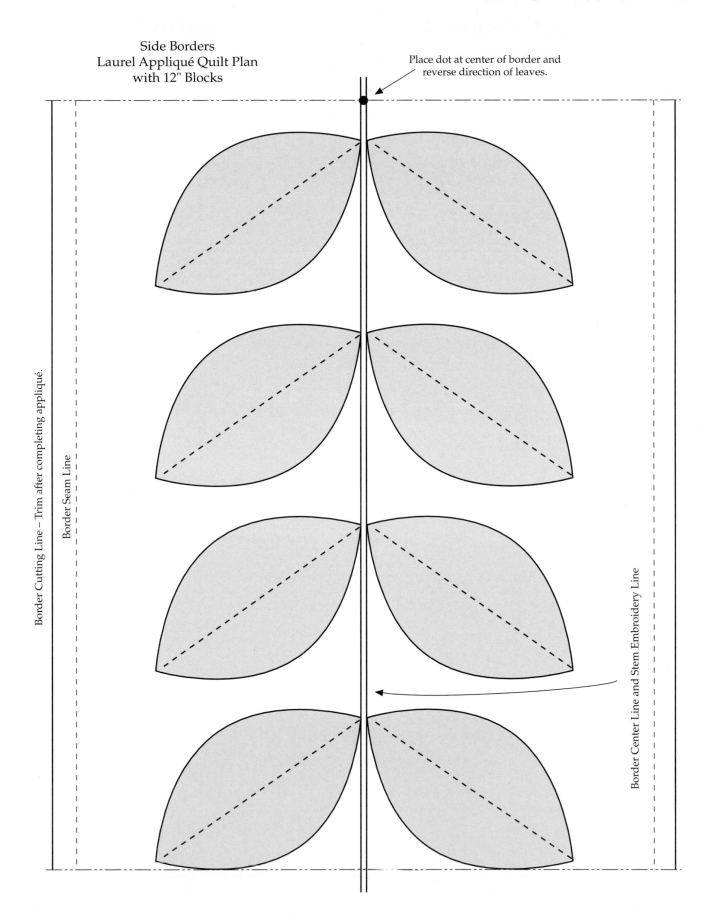

Side Borders
Laurel Appliqué Quilt Plan
with 12" Blocks

Place dot at center of border and
reverse direction of leaves.

Border Cutting Line – Trim after completing appliqué.

Border Seam Line

Border Center Line and Stem Embroidery Line

Leaf Wreath Quilting and Appliqué Motif

This wreath fits a 6" block. Enlarge 200% for a 12" block.

Reversing the Design: This wreath appears as shown in the quilting design in Celestial Navigation (page 76). For appliqué with fusing web (method 1), the design will appear in reverse if traced directly from this version–the leaves will rotate counterclockwise as in Waste Not, Want More (page 35). Make a reverse copy to use as a placement guide.

For appliqué with freezer paper (method 2), make a reverse copy for tracing the wreaths if you want to have them rotate counterclockwise. Use the reverse copy as a placement guide as well.

Use the dotted lines to center the design.

Center Blocks

6" blocks: seam line

12" blocks: enlarge pattern 200% and use this seam line.

Side Half-Blocks

Placement Line

6" blocks:
seam line

12" blocks: enlarge pattern 200%
and use this seam line.

Corner Quarter Blocks

Placement Line

Lesson Plans

These versatile quilt plans may be used to teach a variety of quiltmaking techniques, including basic piecing, paper piecing, and machine appliqué. Teachers and shop owners are welcome to develop classes using this book as a textbook. Please remember that the book's copyright prohibits photocopying or other printing of any materials herein for commercial use. Pages with foundations, quilting, or appliqué designs (pages 105–125) may be photocopied for personal use.

One-Day Workshop

Students learn to piece the basic Eight-Pointed Star block or one of the variations. Have students cut the background fabric triangles in advance to allow more class time for piecing instruction. Review the quilt assembly steps at the end of the workshop.

Recommended Projects: Checkerboard, Night and Noon, and Diamond Border Quilt Plans.

Two Three-Hour Classes

Session 1. Students learn the piecing method used for their star block.

Session 2. Cover any additional techniques used to complete the quilt top, such as alternate block piecing or appliqué.

Recommended Projects: On Point, Laurel Appliqué, Stargazer, or Swallowtail Quilt Plans.

Four Two-Hour Classes

This longer format allows more time for help with design and fabric selection decisions.

Session 1: Demonstrate the piecing method used for the stars. Assist students in choosing a Quilt Plan and customizing it if desired. Discuss fabric selection.

If possible, students should cut the background fabric triangles and star point fabrics before the second session.

Session 2: Students learn the piecing method used for their star block.

Session 3: Students continue piecing star blocks. Cover any additional techniques used to complete the quilt top, such as alternate block piecing or appliqué.

Session 4: Students continue piecing the quilt top. Discuss quilting and finishing options.

Recommended Projects: Any of the designs in the book. Larger projects may require more sewing at home between classes.

Bibliography & Sources

Bibliography

Magic Stack-n-Whack™ techniques
> Reynolds, Bethany. *Magic Stack-n-Whack™ Quilts*. American Quilter's Society, Paducah, KY, 1998.

Machine quilting techniques
> Noble, Maurine. *Machine Quilting Made Easy*. That Patchwork Place, Bothell, WA, 1994.
> Walner, Hari. *Trapunto by Machine*. C&T Publishing, Lafayette, CA, 1996.

Machine appliqué and embellishment techniques
> Roberts, Sharee Dawn. *Creative Machine Arts*. American Quilter's Society, Paducah, KY, 1992.
> Lehman, Libby. *Threadplay*. That Patchwork Place, Bothell, WA, 1997.

Sources

Hancock's of Paducah
3841 Hinkleville Road
Paducah, KY 42001
800-845-8723 or (270) 443-4410
website: http://www.Hancock-Paducah.com
(Quilting fabrics and supplies)

Paper Panache
P.O. Box 2124
Winnetka, CA 91396-2124
website: http://www.paperpanache.com
(Paper piecing patterns and newsletter)

BSR Design, Inc.
P.O. Box 1374
Ellsworth, ME 04605
e-mail: bsrdesign@acadia.net
(Workshops and lectures with Bethany Reynolds)

J.T. Trading Corporation
P.O. Box 9439
Bridgeport, CT 06601-9439
(203) 339-4904
(Basting spray for appliqué and quilting)

PineTree Quiltworks
585 Broadway
South Portland, ME 04106
(207) 799-7357
website: http://www.quiltworks.com
(Quilting fabrics and supplies, including the acrylic Stack-n-Whack™ 45° Cutting Guide; patterns by Bethany S. Reynolds)

This is only a small selection of the books available from the American Quilter's Society. AQS books are known worldwide for timely topics, clear writing, beautiful color photos, and accurate illustrations and patterns. These books are available from your local bookseller, quilt shop, or public library.

#5176 • $24.95

Magic Stack-n-Whack Quilts

#4995 • $19.95

One Block Many Quilts

#5210 • $18.95

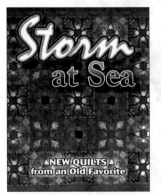

#5592 • $19.95

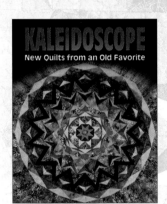

#5296 • $16.95

String Quilts with Style

#5211 • $18.95

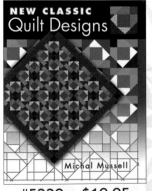

#5339 • $19.95

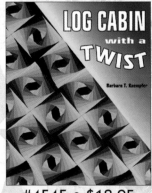

#4545 • $18.95

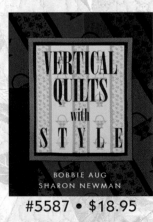

#5587 • $18.95

Look for these books nationally or call
1-800-626-5420.